Weekend Millionaire

Secrets to

Negotiating Real Estate

Also by Roger Dawson and Mike Summey

The Weekend Millionaire's Secrets to Investing in Real Estate
Weekend Millionaire Mindset
Weekend Millionaire Real Estate FAQ

Weekend Millionaire

Secrets to
Negotiating
Real Estate

How to Get the Best Deals to Build Your
Fortune in Real Estate

Mike Summey and Roger Dawson

New York   Chicago   San Francisco   Lisbon   London
Madrid   Mexico City   Milan   New Delhi   San Juan
Seoul   Singapore   Sydney   Toronto

1 2 3 4 5 6 7 8 9 0   FGR/FGR   0 9 8 7

ISBN 978-0-07-149657-5
MHID 0-07-149657-2

While we have tried to make everything is this book accurate, please be aware that all 50 states have different real estate laws and that those laws are constantly changing. Even legal interpretations of those laws change constantly. We cannot guarantee the accuracy or completeness of the information in this book. For your own protection, you should consult with local real estate professionals, attorneys, and CPAs before making decisions based on the information in this book.

McGraw-Hill books are available at special quantity discounts to use as premiums and sales promotions, or for use in corporate training programs. For more information, please write to the Director of Special Sales, Professional Publishing, McGraw-Hill, Two Penn Plaza, New York, NY 10121–2298. Or contact your local bookstore.

To my mother, who instilled in me the drive and determination to succeed in whatever endeavor I attempted.

To my sons, Steve, Jason, and Matt, who never liked to ride around looking at houses when they were little, but who now understand that spending a few hours doing so each weekend can really pay off in the long term.

To my longtime attorney, Albert Sneed, who has always been there to play Devil's Advocate when I came up with a new idea and force me to think it through in its entirety.

To my CPA, Gary Mathes, who has kept me out of trouble with the IRS through several audits.

To the many people from whom I have purchased properties over the years. I hope you always found me to be honest and our negotiations to be fair.

Mike Summey

To my darling wife, Gisela, who continues to enrich my life more than fortunes ever could.

To my delightful grandchildren, Astrid and Thomas, and my three children, Julia, Dwight, and John.

To Bruce Mulhearn, an icon in California real estate, who taught me a great deal about real estate, speaking, and life.

To all the real estate investors who willingly share their knowledge and expertise at real estate investment clubs around the country.

Roger Dawson

To our special friends who join us every week on our Monday evening chats.

To our agent, Jeff Herman, who suggested the Weekend Millionaire project to us.

To our editor, Mary Glenn, who shared our enthusiasm.

To Ron Fry, publisher of Career Press books, for permission to use concepts first expressed in Roger Dawson's Career Press books, *Secrets of Power Negotiating, Secrets of Power Negotiating for Salespeople,* and *Secrets of Power Persuasion for Salespeople.*

Mike Summey and Roger Dawson

Contents

Foreword by Carleton Sheets   *ix*

Preface: Investing the Weekend Millionaire Way   *xi*

Chapter 1   Five Things That Make You a Great Negotiator   1

Chapter 2   Information Is Power   11

Chapter 3   Time Pressure Affects the Outcome   23

Chapter 4   Different Negotiating Styles   33

Chapter 5   Dealing with Bank-Owned Properties   39

Chapter 6   How to Find Government-Owned Properties   47

Chapter 7   How to Locate Owners of Property   57

Chapter 8   Negotiations with Real Estate Agents   67

Chapter 9   Beginning Negotiating Gambits   75

Chapter 10   Middle Negotiating Gambits   103

Chapter 11   Ending Negotiating Gambits   135

Chapter 12   Negotiating with People from Foreign Cultures   151

Chapter 13   Understanding Sellers' Personality Styles   159

Chapter 14   The Art of Win-Win Negotiating   171

Chapter 15   Negotiating Offers That Meet the Seller's Needs   179

Chapter 16   Twenty Closing Tactics   189

Index   *211*

Foreword

Whether you're a new investor trying to learn some extremely effective negotiating techniques or a seasoned pro looking to hone your skills and even learn some new ones, this book is for you.

Everyone knows that recognizing substance over form is vital when evaluating real estate as an investment, but there is absolutely nothing wrong with leading a seller (or buyer, if you're the seller) to seeing a half glass of water as half full rather than half empty. The basis of all good negotiating techniques is perception ... leading a seller to perceive any situation as you would wish him or her to perceive it.

It's like the old story of a person ordering a pizza and when asked if he wants it cut into six or twelve pieces, he responds by saying, "Please just cut it in six pieces; I'm not that hungry."

If success can be measured by the number of times that you buy or sell a property on *your* terms and *your* conditions, you are in for a wonderful surprise. With this book, you will soon rate yourself as an extremely capable and astute negotiator. Perhaps you won't be ready as a hostage negotiator, but you'll be over-ready for real estate transactions.

The huge success Mike Summey and Roger Dawson have enjoyed as real estate investors is largely due to their knowledge of negotiating—to understanding that not everyone wants the same thing from a transaction. Their success as authors comes from writing from first hand experiences, not from researching and reporting on what others have done.

This is the fourth book in the Weekend Millionaire series, and like the first three, it is easy reading that gives practical, real-world advice. The sheer size of many real estate transactions is enough to frighten some people, but when studied and followed, the information contained in this book will turn even the most novice investor into a confident and secure buyer.

I've had nearly 40 years of personal experience and taught thousands of others how to make millions investing in real estate, yet I continue to be amazed by the simple, practical way Mike and Roger are able to put sophisticated investing techniques into laymen's language that anyone can follow.

This book is filled with ideas that will make you money. After reading the manuscript, I picked up a few ideas that I can't wait to put into practice myself, which brings to mind the fact that we never stop learning. So, don't stop here, read the rest of the book and see if you don't agree.

Carleton Sheets

Preface

Investing the Weekend Millionaire Way

When a single book leads to a series of books and multiple other products, it's helpful to have some history and an explanation of how all the different elements fit together. This is our fourth book on investing the Weekend Millionaire way, so let's start by letting you know how we have arrived at this point.

Our first book in the *Weekend Millionaire* series was released in the fall of 2003, when the real estate market was red hot, money was cheap, and gurus were coming out of the woodwork pitching a wide array of schemes for getting rich quick with real estate. Roger is a professional speaker on the topic of negotiating and the former president of one of California's largest real estate firms. Mike is an investor who has been buying income-producing properties for more than 35 years. In *The Weekend Millionaire's Secrets to Investing in Real Estate*, we combined our vast, but different, knowledge to produce a book that taught new investors how to build wealth sensibly with real estate.

Although our experience differed, both of us agreed that the euphoria of the boom years would not last. We have experienced several previous cycles in the real estate market, and we know that bust years invariably follow the booms. Throughout 2007, real estate lost much of its luster as the sales market cooled and problems created by subprime lenders put thousands of people at risk of losing their homes. This bodes well for people investing the Weekend

Millionaire way, because the harder it becomes to sell properties, the more flexible sellers become, and this improves long-term investors' ability to find discounted deals.

As the readers of our first book learned, we don't paint unrealistic pictures, nor do we try to attract students with the lure of quick riches. The "secret" we reveal is that even ordinary working people can build wealth through real estate if they use tried and proven investment strategies and have patience. When the sales market booms, as it did from 2002 until 2006, it is difficult to find deals. Buying one or two properties a year during boom times is very acceptable; however, if you have the patience to wait until conditions change and the market cools, the same effort may result in 10, 20, 30, or even more purchases.

When we wrote that first book, we simply wanted to share the knowledge that has brought us success in the hope that it would help others improve their financial futures. We had no idea that it would lead to an entire series of books and keep us writing for years. As we kick off this fourth *Weekend Millionaire* book, let us tell you about the evolution of the series and how it led to the development of additional products that work together to give you everything you need to become a successful real estate investor.

Many real estate gurus earn their living by selling books and CDs, giving seminars and boot camps, and selling expensive coaching programs, with very little of their income coming from doing what they talk about. Mike has lived solely on the income from his investments for more than a decade. Both of us live very comfortable lives without having to worry about the income from our books or other products. For this reason, we have no reason to withhold information about our investing method in order to entice you to spend thousands of dollars on boot camps and coaching programs. We give you everything you need to be successful, and we do so with very economically priced books and other products. Our method of investing is simple. It is rooted in common sense, and it doesn't have to rely on gimmicks or anomalies in the market to work.

Ralph Waldo Emerson said, "Common sense is genius dressed in its working clothes." He also said, "Society is always taken by surprise at any new example of common sense." We prefer to think that common sense must be a very uncommon thing because so many people have told us that they can't believe investing in real estate can be so simple—that is, until they try our methods and find that they really do work.

We believe that one of the biggest injustices successful people can do to their fellow human beings is to take with them to their graves the knowledge that brought them success and leave behind only what they accumulated. We don't claim to be all-knowing geniuses when it comes to real estate, but we do know that ordinary working people can enjoy tremendous financial success if they learn to use common sense and have patience.

Mike jokingly says that he has a Ph.D. from the University of Hard Knocks, and Roger, who was born in England, literally "came over on the boat." We have gained the knowledge that we share bit by bit by doing what we talk about and write about. Our Weekend Millionaire method of investing has worked for us for decades, and it will continue to work for decades to come because it is rooted in common sense. Unfortunately, with the "have to have it now" mentality that is sweeping this country, only a few people will have the patience to follow the program long enough to realize true success.

This brings us to the reasoning behind the second book in the series, *Weekend Millionaire Mindset: How Ordinary People Can Achieve Extraordinary Success*. Within weeks of our first book hitting the store shelves, we began getting e-mails and letters that, although worded differently, all said the same thing: "Wow, this seems so simple, but how do you develop the right mental attitude to do it?" We had assumed that if we laid out our methods in a simple, easy to understand way, people would, as the Nike ad says, "Just Do It!"

Preface

We kept getting comments like, "I see how this can work, but I just can't bring myself to get started." Or, "I'm afraid I might make a mistake." These comments caused us to look inward and ask ourselves what there was in our backgrounds that enabled us to accomplish what we have been able to achieve. Neither of us had a teacher or a mentor to hold our hand and guide our way. We made mistakes, but we overcame our fears and fumbled our way to success. Why?

We began to realize that we had been able to do something that few people seem to be able to do. We were able to extract the life lessons embedded in our experiences, both good and bad, and use them to create a mindset for success. We developed an "I know I can do it" attitude, instead of an "I hope I can" or an "I wish I could" attitude. It's one of those common-sense things called a positive attitude. In *Weekend Millionaire Mindset*, we weave together stories that show our readers how we pulled these life lessons from different experiences. Several times throughout the book, we encourage people to make notes if reading our stories triggers thoughts about events and experiences in their past.

No two people have the same life experiences. In the final section of *Weekend Millionaire Mindset*, we encourage readers to get out their notes, and we show them how they can develop a personal "Millionaire Mindset" from their own experiences. We discuss key elements like creating desire, eliminating excuses, and getting started. With the publication of this book, we thought we had finally given students both the knowledge and the motivation they needed if they were to become successful wealth builders.

We even designed and minted a beautiful reminder coin that has the look and feel of real gold. Available on our Web site at *www.weekendmillionaire.com*, this coin gives students something that they can carry in their pocket or purse so that if their "thinking starts stinking," they can pull it out and be reminded that they must maintain "The Right Mindset" if they want to become a Weekend

Millionaire. The coins are beautiful and make excellent conversation pieces, especially when you use them to mark your golf ball on the green. The front of the coin reads "The Right Mindset" around the top and "Weekend Millionaire" around the bottom. On the reverse is an eagle with its wings spread, and it reads "United States of America—One Million Dollars." Of course, we had to put the disclaimer "Not Legal Tender" in between the eagle's wings. The coin contains our Web site in small letters just above "One Million Dollars." Check out the coin on our Web site, but keep in mind that the picture doesn't do justice to its beautiful gold color.

The popularity of *The Weekend Millionaire's Secrets to Investing in Real Estate* also brought a request for an audio program from students who wanted to listen to it in their vehicles as they were driving. We know that some people learn better by reading and others learn better by listening, but everyone learns more quickly and retains more when he or she does both. We teamed with Nightingale-Conant and produced *The Weekend Millionaire Real Estate Investing Program.* This eight-hour program on eight CDs, with a printable workbook that is also on CD, allows you to hear us describe the Weekend Millionaire real estate investing method. The time-coded CDs will allow you to hear what you are supposed to be doing while you are actually doing it. You will also get to experience Mike's southern accent and Roger's English accent.

As another way of giving back, and to provide additional support, we began hosting live online chats each week on our Web site. Anyone who is interested in real estate investing, wealth building, or negotiating can join the chats for *free*, ask us questions, and get immediate answers. If you visit our Web site, *www.weekendmillionaire.com*, and register as a "New User," you will get e-mail reminders of the dates and times of the chats. Although we believed that we had been extremely clear in our first two books, we found that people were asking many legitimate questions in the chats. We record the chat transcripts and post them on the Web site so anyone who couldn't participate can go back and read what took place.

After several months of doing this, we realized that another book would be extremely helpful. The live chats move so quickly that it is difficult to give detailed answers to all the questions, so we decided to publish another book. *Weekend Millionaire Real Estate FAQ (Frequently Asked Questions)* groups similar questions and sorts them into chapters that match the chapter titles in *The Weekend Millionaire Secrets to Investing in Real Estate.* In this book, we were able to clarify the questions and give more detailed answers. As a result, the FAQ book became a "must have" companion to the real estate book, but we weren't through yet.

If you summed up the Weekend Millionaire method of investing in a short statement, it would read, "The balancing of price and terms to create wholesale real estate purchases for long-term investment." While that statement is simple to us, we learned that it's not so simple to many other people, especially young people. We discovered that today's schools aren't teaching the basic consumer mathematics that we learned when we were in school. We were amazed at the number of people who didn't know that loan payments are made up of both principal and interest. They didn't understand that there are four parts to a mortgage calculation: loan amount, interest rate, payment amount, and length of the loan. If you know any three of these, you can compute the fourth. When we spoke of balancing price and terms, as we explained it in our books, many people didn't understand what we were talking about.

For long-term investors, there are two factors that determine the value of a property: the amount you pay and how you pay it. For example, a property purchased for $100,000 cash has a different value from one priced at the same amount that can be paid for at $500 per month for 200 months. Rather than writing a math textbook to teach this concept, we teamed with a computer programmer, who happens to be one of our successful students, and developed the "Weekend

Millionaire Offer Generator." This is a software program that does all the work for you. Later, in Chapter 15, "Negotiating Offers That Meet the Seller's Needs," you will learn why this is the best negotiating tool on the market for long-term investors.

We've given you the history of the *Weekend Millionaire* series of books and audio programs; now let's talk about this book. It is the fourth in the *Weekend Millionaire* series, but it may be the most important one of all. You can't make the *Weekend Millionaire* system work if you pay market value for properties and use conventional financing. If you want to make money, you need to understand this important point. Retail merchants can't pay retail for their merchandise and sell it for retail and stay in business. There's no profit! Likewise, long-term investors can't pay market value for properties and rent them at market rates and expect to make a profit. You must buy at wholesale, and that's where the importance of negotiating comes into play.

In this book, we're going to teach you the fine art of negotiating real estate deals. Add this knowledge to the other tools we've developed, and you will have everything you need to meet a seller's needs and be able to conclude a successful negotiation. Contrary to popular belief, negotiating doesn't have to be tense or contentious. In fact, the better you become at negotiating, the easier it will be for you to structure wholesale purchases, and you'll have fun doing it.

In this book, we are going to teach you that negotiating isn't luck, it's an art. You will learn to view it like you would a chess game. There are gambits that can be used in the beginning, in the middle, and at the end of a negotiation that can produce predictable results. If you know and understand them, not only can you use them to your advantage, but, maybe more importantly, you'll know how to counter them if they are used against you. You'll learn about the power that comes from information and time pressure. You'll learn about people from other cultures and how they differ from Americans when negotiating.

You'll also learn how to recognize and deal with people who have different personality styles.

We genuinely want you to be successful, so if you have any questions or just need moral support, don't hesitate to join our live online chats. All of the *Weekend Millionaire* products are available on our Web site, and our books are available in bookstores everywhere. Now let's turn to Chapter 1 and get started.

1

Five Things That Make You a Great Negotiator

An expression that we hear a lot when we are speaking to groups is, "He or she is a born negotiator." We don't think that there is any such thing as a born negotiator. Negotiators are trained, not born. Read the birth announcements in your local newspaper—you'll never see one that says, "At City Hospital today, a negotiator was born." Negotiating is a learned skill. Here are five things that we've noticed about great real estate negotiators.

They Understand That There Is Pressure on the Other Side Too

We all tend to look at things from our own point of view. Sociologists call this *socio-centrism*. This means that we think the person on the other side of the negotiation wants the same things we want. Great negotiators know that what we want has nothing to do with what the other party wants.

For example, we teach that there are many sellers out there who do not want cash for their property. They would prefer to carry back financing and create an income stream. That's hard for some of our beginning students to believe. They assume that all sellers would prefer to cash out. Why do they feel this way? Because that is what they would want if they were selling. What you would want if you were the person on the other side has nothing to do with it. The more you can learn about the seller and the better you understand the seller's true needs, the more chance you have of structuring an offer that will meet those needs.

Another thought that most beginning investors have is this: "The seller doesn't need to sell as much as I want to buy." They always think that they have the weaker hand in a negotiation. Why would that be? The answer is very simple. Investors know all about the pressure that is on them. They don't know about the pressure on the seller. This simple fact always leads investors to believe that they have a weaker hand in the negotiation than they really do. Once you understand this phenomenon and believe it, you become a more powerful negotiator.

Also, we tend to be very conscious of our vulnerabilities. Women at our seminars frequently tell us that they feel disadvantaged because of their gender. Others tell us that they are afraid of rejection. Several people have told us that they feel disadvantaged because of their religious or ethnic background. It's doubtful that any of these perceived vulnerabilities are apparent to the sellers with whom these people are negotiating, but they become an issue when they affect the investor's attitude toward the negotiation.

Great negotiators know that the better they can understand what is driving the other side—what the other person really wants to accomplish—the better they can fulfill that person's needs without taking away from their own position. Poor negotiators get into trouble because they fear that they will be vulnerable to the other side's tricks if they let the other side know too much about them. Instead of trying to find out what is driving the other side and revealing their drives to the other side, poor negotiators let their fears stop them from being that open.

They Practice Negotiating Skills in Inconsequential Situations

Negotiating is a skill, not just knowledge. You can gain knowledge from reading a book, listening to a lecture, or watching an instructional video. A skill you have to learn by doing. It's like a doctor learning how to become a surgeon. She can listen to lectures for weeks. She can stay up all night reading books. But sooner or later she's got to pick up a scalpel and cut someone open. It's the same way with the skill of negotiating—you've got to do it to learn it.

In his seminars, Mike still talks about the day more than 20 years ago that he bought Roger's *Secrets of Power Negotiating* audio program. UPS delivered it to his office just as he was getting ready to go into town to shop at a men's clothing store. He took the program with him and plugged one of the tapes into his car stereo system. The trip into town took about 20 minutes, during which he heard Roger talk about the Flinch Gambit. The idea of having a strong, visible reaction when given a price intrigued him, so he thought, "I'm going to try that and see how it works."

Mike backed up the tape and listened to the technique a second time before he arrived at the store. He was in the market to purchase a new business suit, so he spent several minutes looking through the racks of suits and finally settled on a beautiful navy blue Hickey Freeman suit. He lifted it from the rack, held it up to the light, and asked the proprietor, "How much?"

With a big smile on his face, the shop owner said, "Mike, that is one of our most beautiful suits, and it's only six hundred and fifty dollars."

"SIX HUNDRED AND FIFTY DOLLARS!" Mike exclaimed. "THAT'S A LOT OF MONEY!"

"Mike, Mike," the shopkeeper replied, lowering his voice. "You are one of my very best customers and I want you to be happy." Then he put his arm around Mike's shoulders and said, "Do you really like the suit?"

"I like it, but not SIX HUNDRED AND FIFTY DOLLARS worth."

"Mike, Mike," he said as he held up the suit. "I want you to be happy. Just because you are such a good customer, if you really like the suit, I'll let you have it today for just $575."

Wow! Mike thought, this Flinch stuff really does work! Then he remembered something else he had heard on the tape: if the person drops the price when you flinch, it's a good time to try the Vise Gambit. This technique is merely saying, "No, you'll have to do better than that," when given a price reduction.

Hmmm! Mike thought. If the Flinch Gambit works that well, why not try the Vise Gambit too? He turned to the shop owner and said, "No, you'll have to do better than that." (The exact same words he'd heard Roger use on the tape.)

To his surprise, the shop owner stroked the suit, held it up to the light, turned it around several times, and said, "This is a very beautiful suit, and I want you to have it. If I give you an exceptional price, will you buy it today?

"That all depends on what you consider an exceptional price," Mike replied.

The shop owner slipped the jacket on Mike and led him in front of a full-length mirror. "Look how beautiful the suit will look on you," he said. "Here, go try on the pants and let's get everything fitted because I'm going to let you have the suit today for just $525."

Before this experience, Mike had never thought of trying to negotiate prices in a retail store. Like many people, he thought the price tags were firm and the only way to get a reduction was to wait for the merchandise to go on sale. He saved $125 in less than five minutes of negotiating and soon learned that virtually everything in life is negotiable.

That's smart thinking. When you hear about a new skill, don't think, "I've got to remember that." Instead, think, "I've got to try that." Our advice: for the next 30 days, negotiate everything you do. If you go into a store to buy a ten-dollar item, see if you can get a dollar taken off because the label is torn, or ask them if they'll match the price at the store down the street. Don't wait until you're trying to buy real estate to learn how to negotiate. Practice with little things first.

Unlike Most Americans, They Are Not Reluctant to Negotiate

Negotiating does not come naturally to most Americans. It is not a part of our culture. We look at the price tag and think that this is the lowest price the merchant will take for the item. The rest of the world thinks that it's the highest price the merchant will take. In many parts of the world, if you offered the seller of real estate his asking price, he would be insulted. Really. He would think, "Stuck-up American! You must think you're too good to negotiate with me."

Americans are focused on reaching agreement quickly and feel that anything that slows down the process is counterproductive. Americans feel that you can trust the other person only after you have an ironclad contract signed. People in other cultures feel that you can trust the other person once you get to know him or her well enough. Americans resist making outrageous initial demands because they think it slows down the entire process. People in other cultures are comfortable making outrageous demands because they feel that it's going to take a long time to reach agreement, so it won't do any harm.

They Concentrate on the Issues

Power negotiators know that they should always concentrate on the issues and not be distracted by the actions of the other negotiators. Have you ever watched tennis on television and seen a highly emotional star jumping up and down at one end of the court? He's protesting every line call and spending a lot of time yelling up at the umpire. You wonder to yourself, "How on earth can anybody play tennis against somebody like that? It's such a game of concentration, it doesn't seem fair."

The answer is that good tennis players understand that there's only one thing that affects the outcome of the game of tennis, and that's the movement of the ball across the net. What the other player is doing doesn't affect the outcome of the game at all, as long as you know what the ball is doing. Therefore, tennis players learn to concentrate on the ball, not on the other person.

When you're negotiating, the ball is the movement of the goal concessions across the negotiating table. It's the only thing that affects the outcome of the game, but it's easy to get thrown off by what the other people are doing, isn't it?

Roger recalls wanting to buy a large real estate project in Signal Hill, California, when he was a real estate broker in the late 1970s. The project consisted of 18 four-unit buildings. He knew that he had to get the price far below the $1.8 million that the sellers were asking for the property, which was owned free and clear by a large group of real estate investors. A real estate agent had brought the property to Roger's attention, so he felt obligated to let the agent present the first offer, reserving the right to go back and negotiate directly with the sellers if he wasn't able to get his $1.2 million offer accepted.

The last thing in the world the agent wanted to do was present an offer at $1.2 million—$600,000 below the asking price—but finally Roger convinced him to try it, and off he went to present the offer. By doing that, the agent made a tactical error. He went to the sellers rather than having them come to him. You always have more control when you're negotiating in your power base than if you go to their power base.

He came back a few hours later, and Roger asked him, "How did it go?"

Five Things That Make You a Great Negotiator

"It was awful, just awful. I'm so embarrassed," he told Roger. "I got into this large conference room, and all of the principals had come in for the reading of the offer. They brought with them their attorney, their CPA, and their real estate broker. I was planning to do the silent close on them." (This is to read the offer and then be quiet. The next person who talks loses in the negotiations.) "The problem was, there wasn't any silence. I got down to the $1.2 million, and they said, 'Wait a minute. You're coming in $600,000 low? We're insulted.' Then they all got up and stormed out of the room."

Roger said, "Nothing else happened?"

He said, "Well, a couple of the principals stopped in the doorway on their way out, and they said: 'We're not gonna come down to a penny less than $1.5 million.' It was just awful. Please don't ever ask me to present an offer that low again."

Roger said, "Wait a minute. You mean to tell me that, in five minutes, you got them to come down $300,000, and you feel bad about the way the negotiations went?"

See how easy it is to be thrown off by what the other people are doing, rather than concentrating on the issues in a negotiation? It's inconceivable to think that a professional negotiator such as an international negotiator would walk out of the negotiations because he didn't think the other people were being fair. He might walk out, but you can bet that this would be a specific negotiating tactic, not because he's upset.

Think about a top arms negotiator who shows up at the White House, and the president says, "What are you doing here? I thought you were in Geneva negotiating with the Russians."

Can you imagine the negotiator saying, "Well, yes, I was, Mr. President, but those guys are so unfair. You can't trust them, and they never keep their commitments. I got so upset, I just walked out." Great negotiators don't do that. They concentrate on the issues, not on the personalities. You should always be thinking,

"Where are we now, compared to where we were an hour ago or yesterday or last week?"

Bill Clinton's first secretary of state, Warren Christopher, said, "It's okay to get upset when you're negotiating, as long as you're in control, and you're doing it as a specific negotiating tactic." It's when you're both upset and out of control that you always lose.

That's why real estate salespeople have this happen to them. They lose a listing. They take it into their office manager, and they say, "Well, we lost this one. Don't waste any time trying to save it. I did everything I could. If anybody could have saved it, I would have saved it."

The office manager says, "Well, just as a public relations gesture, let me give the other side a call anyway." The office manager can often hold the listing, not necessarily because he's any brighter or sharper than the salesperson, but because he hasn't become emotionally involved with the people the way the salesperson has. Don't do that. Learn to concentrate on the issues.

They View the Word *No* as Only an Opening Negotiating Position

One thing that we both firmly believe is that the word *no* is not a refusal. It's only an opening negotiating position. When you make an offer to buy at way below what the seller is asking and she explodes with rage at such a low offer and tells you to leave the property right now, this is not a refusal. To a great negotiator, it is only an opening negotiating position.

Take a lesson from your children on this one. You can say to your child, "I am sick to death of hearing about this! Go to your room! I don't want to see you again until tomorrow, and if you ever bring this up again, you're grounded for a month!" Does the child hear this as a refusal? Of course not. He's up on his bed thinking, "Wasn't that an interesting negotiating position?"

Five Things That Make You a Great Negotiator

Mike once had his buyer's broker bring him what he felt was a good opportunity. It was an apartment complex consisting of 10 buildings that ranged from two to eight units per building. The asking price for the properties, which were in need of substantial repairs and were filled with undesirable tenants, was $825,000. Mike inspected the complex and determined that it would take more than $1,000,000 to rehab the buildings, but because of where they were located, he saw an excellent opportunity not only to turn the property around, but to end up with an excellent income property when the rehab was completed. He knew that the seller was not in a position to bring the buildings up to code, and he felt it would be very difficult for the seller to find another buyer who had the ability and desire to do so.

Mike prepared an offer of $525,000 that would require the sellers to carry back $170,000 in a second mortgage. His broker presented the offer and got a firm no. The sellers said that another group was also interested in the property, and they wanted to wait to hear from that group before even making a counteroffer. This was in April. In early May, Mike's broker informed him that the sellers had accepted an offer from a group of doctors that was $65,000 more than his offer, with a closing set for 60 days after signing the contract.

Mike said that he completely understood, but to let him know if the sale did not close; he then forgot about the property. In September, his broker called to say that he had received a call from the sellers' broker asking if Mike's offer was still good.

"I thought the deal was supposed to close a couple of months ago," Mike said.

"It was," the broker replied, "but apparently the doctors' group has been having trouble getting financing, and according to the sellers' broker, the group is now asking for another 60-day extension of the contract to get a certified appraisal. The sellers can't wait that long."

"Well," Mike said, "I'm still interested, but not as much as I was in the spring. I've lost the entire summer, and I was planning to get a large portion of the rehab work done before bad weather sets in."

"What would you be willing to do now?" his broker asked.

"I might be willing to give $510,000 for it," Mike said, "if you would be willing to take $10,000 of your commission in a note for three years."

"I don't want to waste any more of your time or mine, so let me give their broker a call to see if he thinks it would be worth making that offer," his broker said.

After explaining the offer by phone, the sellers' broker called back to ask how long it would take Mike to obtain financing if they accepted his offer. Mike replied that he could attach a letter of credit with preapproved financing to the written offer. The offer was accepted, the deal closed, and it made a point that every investor should remember.

Always leave the door open with sellers. Always say, "That's fine. I hope you do get what you're asking, but if you don't, give me a call and we'll talk some more." When you make written offers, be sure to put your contact information on the document so that the sellers will have it if they later decide to reopen negotiations with you.

Key Points to Remember from This Chapter

- The other side has just as much pressure on it as you have on you.
- Practice your negotiating skills in inconsequential situations.
- Americans are reluctant to negotiate because it's not part of their culture.
- Learn to concentrate on the issues, not the personalities.
- The word *no* is only an opening negotiating position.

2

Information Is Power

Although this book is about real estate negotiating, the basic principles are the same whether you're negotiating with your children or involved in international negotiations.

When Bill Richardson, our former ambassador to the United Nations, was asked by *Fortune* magazine what it took to be a good negotiator, the first thing he said was great advice for real estate investors: "You have to be a good listener. You have to respect the other side's point of view. You have to know what makes your adversary tick." When asked how he prepared for a negotiation, he immediately stressed the importance of information gathering:

I talk to people who know the guy I'll be negotiating with. I talk to scholars, State Department experts, and journalists. Before meeting with Saddam Hussein, I relied a lot on Iraq's ambassador to the United Nations. He told me to be very honest with Saddam—not to pull any punches. With Castro, I learned that he was always hungry for information about America. Sure enough, he was fascinated by Steve Forbes and fascinated with the congressional budget impasse. He fancies himself an expert on U.S. politics. With Cedras of Haiti, I learned that he played "good guy, bad guy" frequently.

The more you know about the seller and his or her needs, the better the deal you will be able to put together. Despite the important role that information plays in a negotiation, few investors spend much time analyzing the seller before making an offer. Even people who wouldn't dream of skiing or scuba diving without taking lessons will jump into a negotiation that could cost them thousands of dollars without spending a minute of time gathering information about the person with whom they will be negotiating. Here are some rules that we've developed over the years that make us better gatherers of information:

Rule 1: Don't Be Afraid to Admit that You Don't Know

If you own your present home, think back to when you bought it. How much did you know about the sellers before you made an offer? Did you know why they were selling and how long they had been trying to sell? Did you find out how they had arrived at their asking price? How much did you know about their real needs and their real intentions in the negotiation? Very often even the listing agent doesn't know all this, does he? He was in direct contact with the sellers when they listed the property. However, when asked about the sellers' objectives, he will very often reply, "Well, I don't know. I know they want cash out, so they're not willing to carry back any financing, but I don't know what they're going to do with the cash. I didn't think it was my place to ask."

Information Is Power

In our seminars, we have the students break into teams of negotiators, with some being assigned as buyers and others as sellers. We give them enough information to complete a successful negotiation. In fact, we purposely give each side discoverable strengths and weaknesses. We tell the people on each side that if the other side asks them a question to which they have been given an answer, they may not lie. If one side unearths only half of these carefully planted tidbits of information, that side will be in a powerful position to complete a successful negotiation.

Unfortunately, no matter how many times we drill students on the importance of gathering information—even to the point of assigning 10 minutes of the negotiation for doing only that—they are still reluctant to do a thorough job.

Why are people reluctant to gather information? Because to find things out, you have to admit that you don't know, and most of us are extraordinarily reluctant to do that.

Here's a quick exercise to prove this point. We're going to ask you six questions. You can answer each of these questions with a number, but instead of having you try to guess the right number, we'll make it easier for you by asking you to answer with a range. If we asked you how many states there are, instead of saying "50," you'd say, "Between 49 and 51." If we asked you for the distance from Los Angeles to New York, you might be less sure, so you'd say, "Between 2,000 and 4,000 miles." You could say from one to a million and be 100 percent sure, of course, but we want you to be 90 percent sure that the right answer falls within the range you give. Do you have the idea? Here are the questions:

1. How many provinces are there in Canada?   Between ___ and ___.
2. How many wives did Brigham Young have?   Between ___ and ___.
3. How much did we pay Spain for Florida?   Between ___ and ___.

4. How many Perry Mason novels
   did Erle Stanley Gardner write?   Between ___ and ___.
5. How many eggs do chickens lay
   each year in the United States?   Between ___ and ___.
6. What was the length of Noah's ark
   in feet, according to Genesis?   Between ___ and ___.

Here are the answers:

1. There are ten provinces in Canada (and two territories).
2. Brigham Young, the Mormon leader, had 27 wives.
3. We paid $5 million for Florida in 1819.
4. Erle Stanley Gardner wrote 75 Perry Mason novels.
5. About 67 billion eggs are laid in the United States each year.
6. Noah's ark was 450 feet long. According to Genesis 6:15, the ark
   was $300 \times 50 \times 30$ cubits, and a cubit equals 18 inches.

How did you do? Did you get them all right? Probably not, but
think how easy it would have been to get them all right. All you would
have had to do was to admit that you didn't know and make the range
of your answer huge. You probably didn't do that because, just like
everyone else, you don't like to admit that you don't know.

The first rule for gathering information is: don't be overconfi-
dent. Don't be afraid to admit that you don't know everything and that
what you do know may be wrong.

Rule 2: Don't Be Afraid to Ask Questions

Don't be afraid to ask questions for fear that one of your questions
might upset the seller. Don't be one of those people who say, "Would
you mind if I asked you?" or "Would it embarrass you to tell me?" Just
ask them:

"How much money do you owe on the property?"
"Are the payments current?"
"Have you had any firm offers yet?"

Information Is Power

"What are you going to do with the money from the sale?"

If the sellers don't want to tell you, they won't. But even if they don't answer the question, you'll still be gathering information. The manner in which they decline to answer a question can often tell you a lot. Act like a good reporter and ask the tough questions. At presidential press conferences, the reporters will say to the press secretary, "When are you going to start bringing the troops home?"

Do they really think that the press secretary is going to say, "I promised the president that I wouldn't tell any of the 500 reporters that keep asking me that question, but since you asked, I'll tell you tell you that we're pulling them out at 2:00 p.m. on Tuesday"? Of course the press secretary isn't going to answer that question, but a good reporter asks it anyway.

Asking the seller the tough questions might put pressure on him or annoy him so much that he blurts out something he didn't intend to. Just judging the seller's reaction to the question might tell you a great deal.

As Roger travels around the country, he's always looking for bargains in real estate. Many years ago (before Florida prices went crazy), he was in Tampa, and he noticed a For Sale By Owner classified advertisement that offered a waterfront home on an acre of land for $120,000. To someone who lives in southern California, as Roger does, this seemed like an incredible bargain. If you could find an acre of waterfront land in California, it would sell for many millions. He called the owner to get more information. The owner described the property, and it sounded even better. Then Roger said, "How long have you owned it?" That's a normal question that very few people would have trouble asking. He told Roger that he'd owned it for three years. Then Roger asked, "How much did you pay for it?" That's a question that many people certainly would have trouble asking. They might think that it would upset the other person and make him angry. There was a long pause on the other end of the line. Finally, the owner responded, "Well, all right, I'll tell you. I paid $85,000." Immediately

Roger knew that this wasn't the great deal that it appeared to be. The real estate market in Tampa had been very flat, and the owner hadn't improved the property.

Roger learned a great deal from asking that one question. If the owner had refused to answer the question, if he had told Roger that it wasn't any of his business what he paid for it, would Roger still have been gathering information? Of course he would. What if the owner had lied to Roger? What if he'd said, "Let's see, what did we pay for it? Oh, yes, we paid $200,000. We're really losing money." If he had lied to Roger like that, would Roger still be gathering information? Of course he would. Don't be afraid to ask the tough questions.

When Roger became president of a large real estate company in southern California, he had to solve the problem of buyers who were not happy with the home they'd bought. The sellers of the home had usually moved out of the area, leaving the company—and Roger—to solve the problem.

Here's what he found was the best way to handle the problem. He would sit the buyers down in his office with a large piece of paper in front of him, and ask, "Please, I would like to know exactly what your complaints are and exactly what you think we should do for you in each instance."

"Well," the buyers would say, "the light switch in the living room doesn't work." Roger would write on the paper, "Light switch in living room." He would continue to ask them if there was anything else until they had aired all of their grievances and he had carefully written them all down on his sheet of paper.

When the buyers ran out of complaints, he would draw a line across the sheet under the last item and show the paper to them. Then he'd negotiate what his company would or wouldn't do for them. Most people are willing to compromise, and if Roger offered to send out a plumber to fix the leaking faucet, in exchange the new owners would be willing to replace the light switch in the living room. With this method, what the buyers wanted was clear from the beginning;

they had laid all of their cards out, face up, and Roger was in the controlling position because he could decide what his response would be.

Most people who handle complaints do it another way, which is foolish. They ask what the problems are and then handle them item by item. The homeowners complain that the light switch doesn't work, and because that's not an expensive item, the person handling the complaint says, "No problem; we'll take care of it." The homeowners immediately think that it will be easy to get more concessions and keep thinking of other things that are wrong. In negotiating terms, that's called escalating the demands. By asking the other person to commit to his or her list of demands first, you put parameters on the size and scope of the problem and establish exactly what is to be negotiated.

If you want to learn about another person, nothing will work better than asking direct questions. We've met only a few people who were seriously averse to answering even the most personal questions. For example, not many people get offended when you ask them, "Why were you in the hospital?"

It's a strange fact of human nature that we're very willing to talk about ourselves, yet we're reticent when it comes to asking other people about themselves. We fear the nasty look and the rebuff we may get if we ask a personal question. We refrain from asking because we expect the response, "That's none of your business." Yet how often do we respond that way to others?

As president of the real estate company in California, Roger wanted to encourage his agents to knock on doors searching for leads. Real estate people call this farming. He found that his agents were very reluctant to do it. He eventually formulated a plan where he would take each one of his 28 office managers out separately, knocking on doors and playing the information game. Roger would say, "Okay, I'm going to knock on the first door, and I'm going to see how much information I can get from these people. You knock on the second door—see if you can get more information than I did."

It was amazing to see the amount of information that people would volunteer to a stranger on their doorstep. Roger could get them to tell him where they worked, where their wives worked, sometimes how much money they made, how long they'd been in the property, how much they paid for it, how much their loan payments were, and so on. People are often eager to volunteer information if we'll only ask.

In our book *The Weekend Millionaire's Secrets to Investing in Real Estate,* we talk about identifying and farming selected neighborhoods in which you would like to invest. Mike has several such neighborhoods that he rides through on a regular basis. He stops and talks with people he sees out in their yards or walking for exercise. Over the years, this practice has resulted in his locating and purchasing several properties that never went on the market. The information he learned from neighbors about pending divorces, job losses, accidents, retirements, and other such situations have given him a wealth of information that he could use to contact owners who had a need to sell.

Asking for more information in your dealings with sellers not only will help you to be a better negotiator but will serve the sellers also, because it will allow you to structure your offers to better meet their needs. We know that the better the job you are able to do in meeting the seller's needs, the more properties you will be able to purchase.

Rule 3: Ask Open-Ended Questions

What's the best way to ask questions? Rudyard Kipling talked about his six honest serving men. He wrote,

I keep six honest serving-men
(They taught me all I knew);
Their names are What and Why and When
And How and Where and Who.

Information Is Power

Of Kipling's six honest serving-men, *Why* is our least favorite. Use it with caution, as Why can easily be seen as accusatory in certain situations. "Why did you let the loan go into default?" implies criticism. "What did you do when you couldn't make the payments?" doesn't imply any criticism. If you really need to know why, you can often make the question softer by rephrasing it using what instead: "You probably had a good reason for doing that. What was it?" By using Kipling's six honest serving-men to form open-ended questions, you'll find out much more of what you need to know.

Closed-ended questions are questions that can be answered with a yes or a no or a specific answer. For example, "Do you plan to retire soon?" is a closed-ended question. You'll get a yes or a no and maybe a date, but that's it. "How do you feel about retiring?" is an open-ended question. It invites more than just a specific answer response.

"Does the sale need to close this month?" is a closed-ended question. "Why do you need to close by the end of the month?" is an open-ended request for information.

Here are four open-ended techniques that you can use to get information.

First, try repeating a comment as a question. Suppose the sellers say, "We want a larger down payment." However, they don't explain why they feel that way, and you want to know why. You repeat the statement as a question: "You want a larger down payment?" Very often, they'll come back with a complete explanation of why they said that. Or if they can't substantiate what they said because they were just throwing it out to see what your response would be, they might even back away from it.

The second technique is to ask for feelings. Don't ask about what happened; instead, ask how someone felt about what happened. The seller says, "We accepted one offer, but the buyer couldn't get the financing." Instead of saying, "What caused that?" try saying, "How did you feel about that?" Maybe the response you get will be, "We were furious. Now we're under a lot of time pressure to get this sold, since otherwise we can't close on our new home."

The third technique is to ask for reactions. The banker says, "The loan committee usually requires a personal guarantee when making loans to LLCs (limited liability companies)." Instead of assuming that this is the only way to get the loan, try saying, "And what's your reaction to that?" The banker may come back with, "I don't think it's necessary, as long as you'll guarantee to maintain adequate net worth in your company. Let me see what I can do for you with them."

The fourth technique is to ask for restatement. The sellers say, "Your price is way too low." You respond, "I don't understand why you say that." Chances are that instead of repeating the same words, they'll come back with a more detailed explanation of the problem. Mike once made an offer that the sellers rejected, saying that his offer was not enough. When he said, "I don't understand why you say that, because I thought it was a very fair offer," the sellers replied that they needed more cash out of the deal than he was offering. This prompted him to ask how much more cash they needed.

The sellers then proceeded to tell him that they had gotten themselves into debt with their credit cards, and that one of the reasons they were selling the property was to get out of debt. They said his offer was $15,000 short of enough cash to pay off their debts. By gathering this information, Mike was able to meet their needs for the additional cash, and in exchange was able to negotiate the sales price down by an additional $5,000.

Let's recap the four open-ended techniques for gathering information.

1. Repeat the question: "You don't think the offer is fair?"
2. Ask for feelings: "And how do you feel about that policy?"
3. Ask for reactions: "What was your response to that?"
4. Ask for restatement: "You don't think we'll get it done on time?"

Rule 4: Where You Ask the Questions Makes a Big Difference

The location where you do the asking can make a big difference. If you meet with people at their real estate broker's office, surrounded by the trappings of power and authority and the formality of doing business, you're least likely to get information.

People in a more formal work environment are always surrounded by invisible chains of protocol—what they feel they should be talking about and what they feel they shouldn't. That applies to executives in their offices, it applies to salespeople on sales calls, and it even applies to a plumber fixing a pipe in your basement. When people are in their work environments, they're cautious about sharing information. Get them away from their work environments and information will flow much more freely. Sometimes all it takes is to get sellers to meet you at a nearby restaurant for a cup of coffee. Often this relaxes the tensions of the negotiation and allows information to flow more easily. For you, if you can meet for lunch at your country club, surrounded by your trappings of power and authority, with the sellers psychologically obligated to you because you're buying the lunch, that's even better.

We think of the information-gathering process as similar to the game of battleship that children play. Children sit at the table across from each other and build a barrier between them so that they can't see the piece of paper that is in front of the other person. Each of them takes a piece of paper and draws a hundred different squares marked with the alphabet down one side and numbers along the bottom. On this graph, they draw their fleet of battleships, cruisers, and destroyers. Then they attempt to bomb each other's fleets by calling out the graph number. When they make a successful hit, they mark the position on their chart, and in doing so they gradually build up a picture of the other person's hidden fleet.

The parallel here is that the hidden piece of paper in negotiations is the other side's hidden agenda. By judicious questioning, you should try to find out as much as you possibly can about that hidden agenda and recreate it on your side so that you know exactly where the people on the other side are coming from and what they're trying to achieve.

Good negotiators always accept complete responsibility for what happens in the negotiations. Poor negotiators blame the other side for the way they conducted themselves. There are no unreasonable sellers out there. There are only sellers that you don't yet know enough about to be able to structure an offer that meets as many of their needs as possible.

There are so many situations that produce good opportunities for investors that you would never have enough money to buy them all even if you knew about them. What frequently happens is that someone else beats you to an opportunity because you are reluctant to ask questions and learn about the sellers' situations. Ask the questions, gather the information, and don't worry about offending the sellers. Keep in mind that you'll never be able to help them unless you know what they need.

Key Points to Remember from This Chapter

- Be a good listener.
- Understand the importance of gathering information about the sellers and their needs.
- Don't be afraid to admit that you don't know.
- Don't be afraid to ask questions.
- Ask open-ended questions.
- Where you ask the questions makes a big difference.

3

Time Pressure Affects the Outcome

Time pressure is an enormous pressure point in getting sellers to give you a good buy. This is even stated in the classic definition of value:

> *A property is worth what a willing buyer will pay a willing seller when both are informed and neither one is under pressure.*

Let's take a closer look at that definition. *Willing* means that the buyer wants to buy and the seller wants to sell, and that neither of them is being forced to do so because of circumstances such as a government agency wanting to condemn the property or confiscate it for the public good. Both the buyer and the seller are *informed*, which means that they are aware of property values in the area. And *pressure* means time pressure, even though it is not specifically defined as such.

What time pressure might sellers be under? Here are just a few:

- They can't afford to make the payments, and they are drifting toward foreclosure.
- They have moved out of town and can't afford double mortgage payments.
- They can't afford the down payment on their new home until they've sold the old one, and the clock is ticking.
- They want to relocate before the beginning of the school year.
- The seller of their next home is putting pressure on them to close.

How much time pressure is the seller under? Time pressure is always a big part of a real estate transaction. If you were to list a property for sale with a broker and you asked the broker how much it would sell for, she would probably say, "How quickly do you want it sold? I can give you a 30-day price, a three-month price, a six-month price, and a one-year price." If you're willing to wait a year, you might get 25 percent more for the property.

When you're dealing with a seller, this is a major factor in how flexible he or she will be on price. A big part of your information gathering should be to find out all you can about the time pressure the seller is under. You'll do a lot better in the negotiation if you know this.

Time pressure also plays a big part in how flexible the seller will be if problems arise before the sale closes. Vilfredo Pareto never studied the time element in a negotiation, yet the Pareto principle reveals the incredible pressure that time can put on a negotiation. Pareto was an economist in the nineteenth century. Born in Paris, he spent most of his life in Italy, where he studied the balance of wealth as it was distributed among the populace. In his book *Cours d'économie politique*, he pointed out that 80 percent of the wealth of Italy was concentrated in the hands of 20 percent of the people.

The interesting thing about the 80/20 rule is that it surfaces repeatedly in apparently unrelated fields. Schoolteachers tell us that 20 percent of the children cause 80 percent of the trouble. In our seminars, 20 percent of the students ask 80 percent of the questions. In real estate negotiations, we say that 80 percent of the concessions will come in the last 20 percent of the time allowed for the negotiation.

Let's say that you sign a contract to purchase a rental property and agree that the closing will take place in 10 weeks. Your offer is subject to your approval of a home inspection report. That's when the trouble starts. The inspection reveals that the roof needs to be replaced. The seller doesn't agree with the report, saying that it's a 25-year roof and it's been on the house for only 20 years. In the seller's mind, the roof has 5 years left on it. This is where the Pareto principle comes into play. If you bring up this problem during the first 80 percent of the negotiating time, it's unlikely that the seller will agree to pay for replacing the roof, which may cause the transaction to fall through. If you wait until the last 20 percent (the final two weeks) to bring up the problem, the seller will be much more likely to go ahead with the repair rather than lose the sale.

Once you understand time pressure, you will know that you should never reveal to the other side that you have a time deadline, but should work to establish that the seller is under time pressure. The only exception to this rule would be if you have all the options and the other side has none. In that case, you might put pressure on the seller by saying, "My partners have told me that unless I put this deal together before the weekend, they want to go ahead and purchase the other property we've been considering."

What to Do When Both Sides Are Approaching the Same Time Deadline

An interesting question is raised when both sides are approaching the same time deadline. This would be true if you're a real estate broker and you lease your office space, for example. Let's say that your five-year lease is up in six months, and you must negotiate a renewal with your landlord. You might think to yourself, "I'll use time pressure on the landlord to get the best deal. I'll wait until the last moment to negotiate with him. That will put him under a great deal of time pressure. He'll know that if I move out, the place will be vacant for several months until he can find a new tenant." That seems like a great strategy until you realize that there's no difference between that and the landlord's refusing to negotiate until the last minute to put time pressure on you.

Here you have a situation in which both sides are approaching the same time deadline. Which side should use time pressure, and which side should avoid it? The answer is that the side with the most power can use time pressure, but the side with the least power should avoid time pressure and negotiate well ahead of the deadline. Fair enough, but which side has the most power? The side with the most options is the one with the most power. If you can't reach a negotiated renewal of the lease, then which of you has the best alternatives available?

To determine this, you might take a sheet of paper and draw a line down the middle. On the left side, list your options if you are unable to renew the lease. What other locations are available to you? Would those locations cost more or less? How much would it cost you to move the telephones and print new stationery? Would customers be able to find you if you moved?

On the right side of the page, list the landlord's options. How specialized is this building? How hard would it be for the landlord to find a new tenant? Would another tenant pay more, or would the landlord have to rent it for less? How much would have to be spent on improvements or remodeling to satisfy a new tenant?

Now you must do one more thing. You must consider the fact that whichever side of the negotiating table you're on, you will always think you have the weaker hand. You know all about the pressure that's on you, but you don't know about the pressure that's on the landlord. Learn to compensate for the feeling that you have the weaker hand. When you list each side's alternatives and you conclude that the landlord has more alternatives than you do, it may only be because you don't know about all the pressure that's on the landlord.

If the landlord actually does have more alternatives than you do, then he's the one with the most power. In this case, you should avoid time pressure and negotiate the lease renewal with plenty of time to spare. However, if you clearly have more alternatives available to you than the landlord does, you may do better in the negotiation by waiting until the last moment and putting him under time pressure.

In our seminars, we set up exercises so that the students can practice negotiating. They may have 15 minutes to complete a negotiation, and we impress on them the importance of reaching agreement within that time. As we walk around the room eavesdropping on the progress of the negotiations, we can tell that during the first 12 minutes, they have trouble making any progress. Both sides tend to stonewall the issues, and we see very little give and take. At 12 minutes, with 80 percent of the time used up, we take the microphone and tell them that they have only 3 minutes left. Then we continue making periodic announcements to keep the time pressure on them, ending with a countdown of the seconds from five to zero. It's very clear that they make 80 percent of the concessions in the last 20 percent of the time available to negotiate.

Your children know about time pressure, don't they? When do they ask you for something? Just as you're rushing out the door, right? Your child is home from college for the weekend and needs money for books. When will he ask you for it? Just at the last minute, when he's racing out the door to head back to school.

We're not saying that children are manipulative, but instinctively, over all those years of dealing with adults, they have learned that people become more flexible when they are under time pressure.

When Negotiations Drag On, People Become More Flexible

The longer you can keep the other side involved in the negotiation, the more likely it is that the other side will move around to your point of view. The next time you're in a situation where you're beginning to think that the other side will never budge, think of the tugboats in the Hudson River off Manhattan. A tiny tugboat can move that huge oil tanker around if it does it a little bit at a time. However, if the tugboat captain were to back off, rev up the engines, and ram the tanker to try to force it around, it wouldn't do any good. Some people negotiate like that. They reach an impasse in the negotiations that frustrates them, so they get impatient and try to force the other side to change its mind. Think of that tugboat instead. It can move the liner around a little bit at a time. With enough patience, you can change anybody's mind a little bit at a time.

Unfortunately, this works both ways. The longer you spend in a negotiation, the more likely you are to make concessions. You may have traveled to your state capital to negotiate a large property acquisition from a corporate owner. At 8 o'clock the next morning, you're in the seller's office feeling bright, fresh, and determined to hang in there and accomplish all of your goals. Unfortunately, things don't go as well as you hoped. The morning drags on without any progress, so you break for lunch. Then the afternoon passes, and you've reached agreement on only a few minor points. You call your family and tell them that you won't be home for dinner. You break for supper and come back determined to get something done. Look out. Unless you're very careful, by 10 o'clock you'll start making concessions that you never intended to make when you started out that morning.

Why does it work that way? Because your subconscious mind is now screaming at you, "I can't walk away from this empty-handed after all the time and effort I've spent on it. I have to be able to put something together." Any time you pass the point where you're no longer prepared to walk away, you have set yourself up to lose in the negotiations. You should ignore any time or money that you have invested in a project up to the present. That time and money are gone whether you strike a deal or not. Always look at the terms of a negotiation as they exist at the moment and think, "Forget about all the time and money I've poured into this deal up to now; should I go ahead with it?" Never be reluctant to pull the plug at any time if the deal doesn't make sense any more. It's much cheaper to write off the time you have invested than it is to plow ahead with a deal that isn't right for you. Be careful not to let time pressure make you too flexible.

That's one of the things that makes Donald Trump such a powerful negotiator—he's not afraid to pull the plug on a deal that no longer makes sense. For example, he spent $100 million to acquire the site for a project on the West Side of Manhattan. It was to be a huge multipurpose commercial and residential site, with 7,600 apartments and a regional shopping mall. He spent millions more developing plans for the project that would include a 152-story tower, the world's tallest. However, when he couldn't negotiate the right tax concessions from the city, he took another look at it and thought, "This was a great project two years ago. It was a terrific project five years ago. It's not a good project in today's market." He shelved the entire project, hoping that the market would revive later and enable him to restart it, which it did. The project is a huge success and will have paid for itself within 10 years of its completion in 2008. You have to look at a negotiation in the same way. Forget what you've already invested and examine whether the deal stills looks good the way things stand now.

On a much smaller scale, Mike once tried to purchase a building in Anderson, South Carolina, in which to locate an office for his advertising company. The owner of the property was a car dealer who prided himself on being a hard negotiator. When Mike made an offer for the property, the owner countered with a price that was nearly three times the amount Mike had offered. They negotiated back and forth for almost a year, but they were still far apart when Mike walked away from the negotiations and purchased another property instead.

When the car dealer heard that Mike had bought another property, he called him and said, "I thought you wanted to buy my property. I would have been willing to come down a good bit more on the price, but I was waiting to see if I could get you to come up some more."

Mike told him that he would have preferred to have the car dealer's location rather than the one he had bought, but he couldn't wait any longer to get an office established. He told the car dealer that if he ever decided to sell the property at a reasonable price, he might still be interested. He moved forward with refurbishing the property he had purchased and soon had opened an office in it.

Over a year after he was in the new office, he had a visit from the car dealer. "Are you still interested in that property of mine?" he asked.

"I might be," Mike said. "How much are you asking for it?"

"I'll let you have it for the same price that was in that last offer you made me," he replied.

"Well, when I made that offer, I was under pressure to get an office opened, but that's not the case anymore. Now that I have an office, which is working out very well, I don't really need the property anymore. If bought it, it would just be for investment purposes, and I couldn't put anywhere near that much into it," Mike said.

Immediately, the car dealer said, "What if I were willing to sell it for what you originally offered me? Would that interest you?"

"It might," Mike said, "especially if you would finance the purchase and let me pay you interest only for five years."

"I can't do that," he said. "I've had something come up that I need to raise some cash to handle. That's the only reason I'd even consider selling it that cheaply. At that price, I'd have to have all cash, and I'd need to close by the end of the month."

"I'll tell you what," Mike replied. "I don't really need the property, but if you'll knock another 10 percent off the price, I'll not only buy it for cash, I'll close next Friday. How would that work for you?"

The dealer stuck out his hand and said, "Let's shake on it! You've got a deal. Write up the contract and I'll sign it."

Time Pressure Affects the Outcome

This was a classic example of how time pressure can change the entire landscape in a negotiation. In the beginning, the dealer kept holding out, thinking that Mike wanted the property badly enough to be willing to pay almost any price to get it. The fact that they had been negotiating for the better part of a year gave the dealer this impression. When Mike suddenly purchased another property and ended the negotiations, it deflated the dealer's hopes of making a big profit and left him with a property that he really needed to sell. When the deal fell apart, the dealer revealed to Mike that he would have been willing to come down considerably on the price, and Mike let him know that he might be interested at some point in the future if he could purchase the property at a reasonable price. This left the door open for future discussions.

What happened was that the car dealer got into a rather serious financial bind and needed to raise cash quickly. When he called Mike back about the property, the time pressure caused by this problem led him to be much more flexible. As a result, Mike bought the property at a price that was 10 percent below what he had originally offered almost three years before. Since the location was where he had originally wanted to put his office, he renovated the building to fit his needs and moved into it. Then he converted the other building into a good commercial rental property.

Acceptance Time

Another way of using time to your advantage is what negotiators call acceptance time. Your proposal may be abhorrent to the seller initially. There's absolutely no way she will even consider it. But if you can be patient and leave the proposal on the table long enough, the seller may eventually find it acceptable. Negotiators call acceptance time the time it takes for a person to realize that an unacceptable proposal is the best she can do. Here are some examples:

- *Death*. It may be a few decades away, but we all learn to accept it eventually.

- *Hijacking.* The hijacker wants $10 million and a ticket to freedom. He settles for the chance to surrender with dignity.
- *Selling real estate.* We thought we'd get a million dollars for the home we've come to love. After putting it on the market for six months, we reluctantly accept the idea that buyers don't love it as much as we do.
- *College acceptance.* We had our heart set on sending our son to Stanford. We reluctantly accept that, given his grades, he is lucky to get into a community college.

Be aware of the acceptance time phenomenon and be patient. It may take the other side a while to consider your proposal seriously.

Time is comparable to money. They can both be invested, spent, saved, or wasted. Invest the time to go through every step of the negotiation, use time pressure to gain an advantage, and don't yield to the temptation to rush to a conclusion. Good negotiators know that time is money if it is used properly.

Key Points to Remember from This Chapter

- There are three major factors that always affect the outcome of a negotiation: how intimidated you are, how much information you have, and how much time pressure each side is under.
- The price of a property may vary by 25 percent depending on how quickly the seller needs to sell.
- As a rule, 80 percent of the concessions will come in the last 20 percent of the time allowed for the negotiation.
- Problems raised under time pressure are resolved more quickly.
- The side with the most options can make the best use of time pressure.
- When negotiations drag on, people tend to become more flexible.
- Be careful not to let time pressure make you too flexible.
- Appreciate acceptance time. It takes time for sellers to realize that they're not going to get everything they want.
- Time is money if you know how to use it.

4

Different Negotiating Styles

Knowing what is driving the seller's negotiating style is the key to understanding the pressure points that will enable you get a good deal from him or her.

The Competitive Style

This is the style that neophyte negotiators know best, and it's why they see negotiating as being so challenging. Sellers who feel that they have lots of options available to them think that all they have to do to get a good offer from you is to be a tougher negotiator. If you assume that sellers are out to beat you by any means within the rules of the game, of course you will be afraid of meeting people who might be better negotiators than you or who are more ruthless than you.

The competitive style is certainly used at most car dealerships. The car dealer attracts customers by offering "the lowest prices in town" but pays its salespeople based on the amount of profit they can build into the sale. It's a gladiatorial approach to negotiating: the customer wants to buy at the lowest price, even if the dealer loses money and the salespeople make no commission; and the salesperson wants to drive up the price because that's the only way he can make money. It's a type of negotiation where you should sound the trumpets, let the spectacle begin, and may the best person win.

Competitive-style negotiators believe that you should find out all you can about the people on the other side without letting them know anything about you. Knowledge is power, but competitive-style negotiators believe that because of this, the more they can find out and the less they reveal, the better off they'll be.

When gathering information, competitive-style negotiators distrust anything that the other side's negotiators tell them because it might be a trick. They gather information covertly, getting all the information they can about you and your real estate investing style. Since they assume that you are doing the same to them, they work diligently to prevent the leaking of information about themselves that might be of value to you. They may be in default on their mortgage, but they don't want you to know that. They may desperately need to close this sale so that they can complete the purchase of their retirement home, but you're the last person with whom they're going share that information.

What causes this approach is the assumption that there has to be a winner and a loser. It ignores the possibility that both the seller and the buyer could win because they may not be looking for exactly the same thing. By knowing more about the other side, each side can concede issues that are important to the other side but may not be significant to their side.

The Solutional Style

This is the best negotiating situation for a real estate investor. A seller with this style is eager to find a solution to his or her real estate problem and is willing to calmly discuss with you the best way to do that.

This means that nobody's going to threaten the other side and that both sides will negotiate in good faith to find a win-win solution.

Solutional-style negotiators tend to be open to creative solutions because they feel that there must be a better solution that just hasn't occurred to them yet. It takes an open mind to be creative. Just look at some of the variables that buyers and sellers could propose in a transaction as uncomplicated as buying a house:

- The cost of financing could be adjusted by letting the buyer assume an underlying loan (with the lender's permission, of course). Or the seller could carry back all the financing and remain liable for the underlying loan (called "wrapping the underlying")—again with the lender's permission.
- The buyer could accommodate the seller by giving him or her more time to move out or find another home. The seller could even lease back the house from the buyer for an extended term.
- The price could include all or some of the furnishings.
- The sellers could retain a life estate in the house that would enable them to live there until they died. This is a great idea for elderly people who need cash but don't want to move.
- The broker's fee could be eliminated, or the broker could be asked to take his fee in the form of a note, rather than in cash.
- The buyer could move in but delay the closing to help the sellers with their income taxes.

The great thing about negotiating with someone who has the solutional style is that nothing is cast in stone. People with this style are not restricted by thoughts of how real estate is traditionally sold. Short of breaking the law or their personal principles, they will listen to any suggestion you care to propose because they do not see you as being in competition with them.

Having both sides cooperating to find a perfect and fair solution sounds like the ideal situation for a real estate investor, doesn't it? However, there is one caveat: the sellers could be feigning when they appear to be using the solutional style. Once you have put your cards on the table and told them exactly what you are prepared to do, they may revert to the competitive style of negotiating. If the situation seems too good to be true, be wary.

The Personal Style

With this style, personal considerations override what would be in the best interests of the seller and/or the buyer. In our book *The Weekend Millionaire's Secrets to Investing in Real Estate,* Mike described a property he bought that was owned by a man and a woman who had gone through a very antagonistic divorce. Neither one was willing to do anything that would help the other, even if this was to their own detriment. Mike was able to develop a creative solution to buying the house while satisfying the emotional and financial needs of both sellers. He got a great buy, the man got the cash he needed, and his former wife got the price she was insisting on. Even more important, they were able to stop feuding with each other and get on with their lives.

The personal style often comes into play with properties bought out of probate. The relatives who inherited the property may be scattered all over the country and have many different financial needs. Sometimes they're not talking to one another, and their attitude is, "I don't care what we do as long as my deadbeat brother doesn't get anything from it."

The Organizational Style

This style often comes into play when you are dealing with several sellers or when you are buying from an entity such as a corporation, charity, or religious organization. The organization's representative may be comfortable using a solutional style, but he or she knows that in order to sell you the property, it will be necessary to formulate a solution that can be sold to the organization. Whatever style the representative uses to find a solution, it must be presented to the members of the entity he or she represents in an organizational style.

When dealing with someone using the organizational style, you need to be thinking, "Who might be giving the negotiator heartburn over this one?" If it is a corporation, it may be the stockholders, or the legal department, or perhaps government regulations. If it's a church, it may be the congregation or the finance committee. Once you understand the negotiator's problem, you should try to formulate your offer in a way that will make it more palatable to the organization. For example, you might take a more radical position in public than you do at the negotiating table. If you do this, your compromise may give the appearance of making major concession.

A company hired Roger to help it when its assembly workers' union went on strike. The union negotiators felt that the solution they had negotiated was reasonable, but they couldn't sell it to their members, who were out for blood. They developed a solution in which the local newspaper interviewed the president of the company. During the interview, the president expressed sincere regret that he was caught in a difficult situation. The union couldn't sell the plan to its members, and he couldn't sell anything better to his board of directors and stockholders. It appeared that the strike would soon force him to move production from that factory to the company's assembly plant in Mexico. The next day, the workers' spouses opened the newspaper to read headlines that said, "Plant to Close—Jobs Going South." By the afternoon of that day, the spouses had put enough pressure on the workers that they clamored to accept the deal that they had previously turned down.

If you're dealing with someone who has to sell your offer to his or her organization, you should always be looking for ways to make it easier for the person to do so.

The Attitudinal Style

A negotiator with this style believes that if the two sides trust each other and like each other, they can resolve their differences. Attitudinal-style negotiators will never try to resolve a problem by telephone or through an intermediary. They want to be face to face with the other person so that they can get a feel for that person, believing that, "If we know each other well enough, we can find a solution."

The problem with this kind of negotiating is that it can easily lead to appeasement of the other side. The attitudinal-style negotiator is so eager to find good in the other side that he or she can easily be deceived. It helps if both negotiators know and like each other because it's hard to create a win-win solution unless the two sides trust each other. However, good negotiators know that there is something far more important than having the other side like and trust you: you must create a solution that is in the best interests of both sides. When it is mutually beneficial for both sides to support the agreement and see that it is implemented, it doesn't matter whether they like each other or not.

Study these five approaches to negotiating, and after you have gathered as much information about the seller as possible, select an approach that will be most effective based upon the seller's style.

Key Points to Remember from This Chapter

Learn the five styles that motivate a negotiation:
- The competitive style
- The solutional style
- The personal style
- The organizational style
- The attitudinal style

5

Dealing with Bank-Owned Properties

If you've been investing in real estate for any length of time, you've probably seen television infomercials or been exposed to seminar leaders talking about how you can make big money buying bank-owned properties for pennies on the dollar. Don't believe it. Yes, banks want to dispose of properties that they have acquired through foreclosure or from the receipt of deeds in lieu of foreclosure, but they are going to take a loss only as a last resort, not in the normal course of liquidating the properties. When they do get stuck with difficult situations, traditional banks are more willing to cut their losses and move on than thrift institutions, but neither are going to dispose of properties foolishly the way some seminar leaders claim they will.

In today's market, just locating bank-owned properties can be challenging. In the past, most lending institutions would publish lists of foreclosures, and all it took to get on their mailing list was a phone call. Now, with the advent of the Internet, it's a different story. There are about as many different ways of handling bank-owned properties as there are banks. After conducting interviews with the special asset managers at banks ranging in size from small local banks to the largest ones in the country, we discovered that there is no such thing as the right way to locate foreclosed properties. There are commercial Web sites where you can sign up and pay a fee to get what purport to be lists of foreclosures, but we've found that it's just as easy to find the information for free. Much of what you get from these paid sites is gathered from public records and is often outdated.

Our first suggestion is that you visit a bank's Web site. Bank of America has a great Web site where you can find a listing of all its REO (which stands for real estate owned) properties, complete with descriptions and contact information. Several smaller banks also have similar information on their Web sites. Other banks don't offer this information on their Web sites at all. Wachovia Bank, for example, turns all its properties over to the Real Estate Transaction Network; you will find its properties listed at *www.res.net*. Still other banks work with local Realtors® and don't provide any comprehensive listing. Remember that, although their methods may differ, each bank wants to get as much as possible for the properties it has unwillingly taken into inventory.

Nearly all single-family residential and other small properties acquired through foreclosure actions are sold by real estate agents. Occasionally small banks will sell properties directly, but that's the exception rather than the rule. But just because properties are listed with real estate agents doesn't mean that you can't get some good deals. As we mentioned earlier, banks want to get as much as possible for their properties, but as with any other sellers, cash offers with quick closings and no contingencies will always get more consideration than higher-priced offers that are contingent upon financing and delayed closings. If you are able to buy for cash and close quickly, there are some great deals available from all sellers, not just banks.

Dealing with Bank-Owned Properties

Mike recently purchased two houses from a local bank in a transaction that serves as a good example of why cash is considered king in real estate. The bank had originally financed the properties for another investor, who had borrowed more than $80,000 on each one. The tax appraisals on the houses were $102,100 and $103,500, respectively. They were rented for $650 per month each, which was not adequate to cover expenses and make the payments. Eventually the investor fell behind on the payments, and the bank foreclosed.

When Mike learned of the foreclosures, he contacted the bank and expressed an interest in buying the properties. The tenants were still in the houses and were paying their rent directly to the bank. The bank's collections manager arranged a showing of the properties, and when Mike arrived to pick him up, the president of the bank decided to come along as well. Once they were back in his car after going through the houses and conducting an inspection, Mike turned to the collections manager and said, "I'll give you $125,000 for the two of them."

Immediately, the collections manager spoke up and said, "Oh, no, we can't do that. We've got over $80,000 in each of them."

"Well, based on the rents they are bringing in and what I calculate would be the expenses, that's as much as I can pay and make the numbers work," Mike replied.

At this point, the bank president turned to Mike and asked, "Would you need us to finance them for you?"

"Not unless you just want to," Mike said.

"If we sold them for cash, how soon could you close?" the bank president asked.

"How about the day after tomorrow?" Mike replied.

What happened next demonstrates the appeal of a cash offer with a quick closing. The bank president turned to the collections manager, who was in the back seat, and said, "Have you ever heard of a bird in the hand?"

Two days later, the bank had its attorney deliver a deed and title insurance binder to Mike's closing attorney, and Mike wrote a check to conclude the purchase. The fact that this sale occurred so quickly is a testament to the power of cash offers with quick closings. Had Mike offered the same $125,000, but needed to have the bank finance the purchase, there is no way he would have gotten the properties at that price. In fact, had the bank been required to finance the purchase, the collections manager advised that it would not have sold the houses for less than the entire amount it was owed. Remember, cash is king!

Rare exceptions like this have been used as examples to create an entire industry filled with real estate gurus whose television infomercials trumpet how people can become instant millionaires buying foreclosures for pennies on the dollar and then flipping them for huge profits. In fact, one special asset manager Mike spoke with at a large national bank said, "You wouldn't believe the number of people who come in here and sit across the desk from me wanting to buy our foreclosed properties and their fingers are still orange from the Cheetos they were eating the night before when they watched that late night infomercial." We had a good laugh at that one.

Many REO properties are sold at auction by companies like Williams & Williams Marketing Services, Inc. This is one of the country's largest auction companies; you can visit its Web site at *www.williamsauction.com*, where you will find listings of both private and bank-owned properties throughout the United States. Bank-owned properties sold at these auctions are not to be confused with the foreclosure auctions that occur on the local courthouse steps. These are properties that have already been through the foreclosure process, which clears the title of secondary encumbrances. REO properties purchased at these auctions are transferred with clear titles and title insurance.

Dealing with Bank-Owned Properties

It's impossible to predict the price that properties will sell for at auction. You may attend one auction where the property sells at half its appraised value and another where it goes for more than the appraisal. While we were going through the final edits for this manuscript, Mike attended one of these auctions in a neighborhood where he already owns several houses. The price range in that neighborhood was $145,000 to $180,000. The minimum opening bid on the house was $50,000. Mike took his son Matt, and they were prepared to pay up to $150,000 for the house. When the auctioneer started the sale, the bidding was between an older woman and a middle-aged couple.

Quickly the bids went above the $150,000 Mike would have paid and went all the way to $240,000 before slowing down. Eventually the couple gave the winning bid, which together with the auction fee was $259,500. No house in the neighborhood had ever sold for anywhere close to this amount, but what happened was that the two bidders became competitive with each other, and neither of them was about to be outdone by the other. In this case, the house sold for many thousands of dollars above the appraised value and above what anyone would have considered a reasonable retail price.

If you plan to attend one of these auctions and bid on a property, do your homework before you go. We recommend that you use the *Weekend Millionaire Offer Generator* (as Mike and his son did) to calculate the maximum amount you can pay for a property. Be sure to use the option in the program that lets you "calculate a cash offer" because you will be expected to pay cash when you buy at an auction sale. It is rare for financing to be available, even for qualified buyers. If you will need financing to make the purchase, you should have it arranged and preapproved prior to going to the auction.

Don't shy away from auction sales because you are afraid you won't get a deal. In Chapter 16 of *The Weekend Millionaire's Secrets to Investing in Real Estate*, we describe buying an REO property at auction for several thousand dollars less than Mike had offered the bank several months before he bought it at auction. Mike will also tell you that he has attended sales where uninformed, uneducated buyers like the ones described earlier became caught up in the festive and competitive environment created by a charismatic auctioneer and bid the price far beyond what any knowledgeable investor would pay. The best advice we can give you about auctions is to know the maximum you will pay before you go and don't exceed it, no matter how strong the urge to do so becomes.

Recent changes in banking laws have made it more difficult for banks to deal directly with investors when selling REO properties, which is why most institutions now use real estate agents to handle their sales. Unless the sales can be documented as arms-length transactions, banks are under much more scrutiny, especially if they provide financing for a sale. The loans they make in such situations are classified as "loans to facilitate" and are viewed differently from other loans by regulators. Thrift institutions are more able to deal directly with investors because they are not under as much scrutiny as the national banks and may be more inclined to provide financing when selling an REO property.

We realize that locating and buying REO properties can be confusing and frustrating, but you should not overlook the opportunities that they present. Before banks put properties on the market for sale, they get a market appraisal and use it as the basis for coming up with a listing price. Does that mean that they won't take less than their asking price? No.

The appraisals that banks receive are based on the amount an appraiser estimates the properties will sell for if given adequate time and properly marketed. In nearly all cases, banks will use this appraised value as a benchmark to establish what they call an NRV, or net realizable value. This value may be more or less than the loan amount that was foreclosed upon, but once the properties are placed in inventory, they are put on the bank's books at the NRV. If this is less than the amount the bank has in the property, it takes the loss at that point. NRV is the net amount the banks expect to receive after all expenses, including real estate commissions, have been paid. Because of the time value of money, the longer a property is expected to stay in inventory, the lower the NRV is set. For this reason, banks want to sell properties as quickly as possible, so when they are establishing the NRV, they factor in a price reduction that they hope will encourage a quick sale. This may result in their putting the properties on their books at 15 to 40 percent or more below the appraised value, depending on market conditions and other circumstances.

Knowing this information will help you to prepare your offers. Although the listed price may be more than you can pay, banks want to get at least the property's NRV, and more if they can. If they are unable to do this within a reasonable time, they may offer the properties at absolute auction (that's an auction where no upset bids are allowed after the final bid is made) by companies like Williams and Williams Marketing Services, Inc., which we mentioned earlier. At these auctions, the banks agree to accept the high bid, whatever it is. A word about upset bids: As we teach you in the following chapter, when properties are auctioned, there is frequently an upset bid period, usually 10 days, in which your bid can be upset by a bid that is at least 10 percent higher than your bid. In other words, your bid is not final at the auction and is not accepted until the upset period has passed.

While foreclosure opportunities are good, we don't recommend focusing on them any more than you would focus on the dozens of other opportunities where deals can be found. They should be viewed as just another potential prospect to be added to the collection of opportunities you will use in your search for bargains.

Key Points to Remember from This Chapter

- Banks don't want to carry foreclosed properties on their books, but they're not going to give them away.
- Check your local banks' Web sites to see if they list REOs there.
- Check out the Real Estate Transaction Network Web site at www.res.net. This is an auction site that banks use to dispose of REOs.
- If you can pay all cash, this could be an important negotiating tool, even when buying from banks.
- If you buy an REO from a bank, it is postforeclosure and all junior loans will have been cleared from the title.
- Banks are often reluctant to deal directly with you. They prefer to list with a broker so that they cannot be accused of unfair practices.

6

How to Find Government-Owned Properties

You can often find good deals on properties owned by the federal, state, or local government. Why would the Feds or other government agencies own property, and why would it be of interest to you? There are several reasons.

Defaulting FHA loans. One big reason is that the government offers loan guarantees for financing for low-income buyers through the FHA (Federal Housing Administration). When those loans go bad and the properties are foreclosed upon, HUD (U.S. Department of Housing and Urban Development) ends up owning the properties. It fixes them up and puts them back on the market.

Defaulting VA loans. As part of their benefit package, veterans meeting certain requirements are offered low or no down payment loan guarantees and low interest rates. When VA-guaranteed loans default and the government ends up owning the properties following foreclosure, it resells those properties.

Sheriff's sales. About half of the states use this judicial process when foreclosing on mortgages; in addition, law enforcement agencies may confiscate properties from lawbreakers and put them up for sale at auction.

Property tax liens. If owners don't pay their property taxes, the tax lien will eventually be sold to cover back taxes. You can bid to buy that tax lien, but there is usually a period of time, often many years, during which the owner of the property can redeem that property. When this happens, the owner must pay the holder of the tax lien the amount of the lien plus interest.

A word of warning. Before we get into this topic, we need to warn you that the area of government-owned properties tends to attract the worst type of seminar promoters. There is something attractive about the thought of taking advantage of the government. Another universally held belief is that the government would do something stupid like buying $640 toilet seats or giving away property at half its real value. You may have already heard some seminar promoter offering to teach you (for a huge fee) how to take advantage of the government and start raking in huge amounts of money.

Many years ago, a seminar promoter hired Roger to teach negotiating skills to a group of real estate investors in San Francisco. There had been three speakers earlier in the day, and he was the wrap-up speaker. He went down to the ballroom of the hotel to hear the last 15 minutes of one of the other speakers.

There was a table set up in the back of the room where the speaker's audio programs were for sale at $395. Roger took a seat to hear what the speaker had to say and was amazed to see that people were getting up and heading for the back of the room, even though the speaker was still talking.

How to Find Government-Owned Properties

At first Roger thought these people were leaving in protest. But no! They were heading back to buy the speaker's audio programs. As a crowd formed at the table, others in the audience were getting up and hurrying back, evidently afraid that the programs would sell out before they got a chance to buy. Half his audience was back there, and he was still conducting the seminar!

Roger was curious to find out what on earth would cause this kind of hysteria. Later he found out that it wasn't unusual for the seminar leader to sell $50,000 worth of these audio programs at a seminar. Since they were going to repeat the program in Los Angeles the following day, Roger made a point of being at his session to hear his entire presentation.

The speaker was promoting a get-rich-quick scheme that involved using government money to rehabilitate slum property. He was actually suggesting that you could set yourself up as the building contractor and the government would send you all the money you needed. Roger's years as a real estate broker told him that the scheme was unworkable in the real world, even if it was legal—which he seriously doubted. Roger promptly refused to speak on any more programs where this person was going to be one of the other speakers. Later we heard that the Federal Trade Commission had fined the speaker $2.1 million because he was exaggerating the ease with which real estate loans could be obtained.

Mike is frequently asked to speak at real estate investment symposiums, but is very cautious about accepting these engagements for the same reason as Roger. There are so many speakers who claim to be real estate gurus running around the country dispensing bad and often fraudulent advice that Mike is concerned that his image and reputation will be tarnished if he appears to be one of them. As the old Italian proverb says, "Those who sleep with dogs will rise with fleas."

Don't buy into this kind of thinking. As plausible as it may sound to you, people in government are not stupid. When they need to dispose of an asset, they will do everything they can to maximize their return, just like any other seller. There are good buys available from government agencies, but nobody is giving anything away.

With that said, let's take a look at some government programs that can produce foreclosures that might be good buys for you.

FHA Loans

Most people think of FHA loans as being government loans, but they really aren't. The government insures the loan, but the loan is made by a conventional bank or mortgage broker, just like most other loans.

The FHA is a division of HUD. It has been in business since 1934, and it has done a wonderful job of enabling low-income buyers to purchase one- to four-unit buildings with low down payments, low closing costs, and easier standards for getting credit. It's a great program for first-time buyers because the down payment can be as little as 3 percent of the purchase price and closing costs can be added to the loan. The maximum amount of the mortgage depends on the price of housing in your area. You can look it up by typing this link into your browser: *https://entp.hud.gov/idapp/html/hicostlook.cfm*.

Roger checked Los Angeles County recently (where he lives), and found that the maximum was the highest in the mainland United States at $372,790 for a single-family house and up to $697,696 for a fourplex. Add 50 percent to that if you're in Alaska, Guam, Hawaii, or the Virgin Islands.

Mike checked Buncombe County, North Carolina, where he lives, and found the maximum to be a more modest $200,160 for a home and $384,936 for a fourplex.

Can you use an FHA-insured loan to purchase rental property? No, it has to be owner occupied. However, if you are transferred, you can rent out your home and get another FHA-insured loan on your new residence. Roger bought his first four homes that way and turned each one into a rental when he was transferred. He quit his job and went into real estate full time when he realized that he was making more money on his rentals than he was on his job.

VA Loans

If you have served at least 181 days in the military (or half that in wartime) and received a discharge other than dishonorable, you can probably qualify for a VA loan. The Department of Veterans Affairs (VA), not HUD, insures this loan. These loans typically require no money down, and closing costs can be included in the loan. You don't have to be a veteran to assume a VA loan, but the veteran's eligibility to get another VA loan is suspended until the first loan is fully repaid. The maximum loan amount is figured using a complicated formula, but it's roughly $417,000 for the lower 48 states and 50 percent more in Alaska, Guam, Hawaii, or the Virgin Islands.

With that brief summary of government loan guaranty programs out of the way, let's take a look at how you can buy those properties when the borrower defaults.

FHA Foreclosures

When a borrower defaults on an FHA loan, HUD takes back the property and resells it through a network of HUD-approved real estate brokers. These are your regular neighborhood brokers who have gone to the FHA to take the courses that get them certified. Roger did this when he was a broker and still recalls it as one of the most boring days of his life! HUD-approved brokers spruce up the property and suggest a reasonable price for the resale. Buyers then bid on the properties through the approved broker. Preference is given to owner-occupiers by setting aside a time when only bids from owner-occupiers will be accepted. If no offer is accepted during that time, investors can then bid. HUD does not offer financing on these purchases directly, but most lenders will work with HUD homes. All HUD homes are sold as is, so be careful to inspect the property. It's a good idea to make your offer subject to your approval of a home inspection report that you must pay for. Some of these properties get pretty beat up before the defaulting homeowner surrenders them, so be cautious.

Since this is the government we're talking about, it's not that simple. Apart from owner-occupiers, it also gives preference and substantial discounts to law enforcement officers, firefighters, emergency medical technicians, and teachers through its Good Neighbor Next Door Sales Programs. These people must live in the property for three years to earn the discount, but evidently the government thinks that their being there improves the neighborhood.

How do you locate HUD properties for sale? Go to HUD's Web site at *www.hud.gov*.

A word of caution here: there are all kinds of entrepreneurs pretending to be the HUD Web site. For example, *www.hud.com* is a commercial site that sells real estate search information. Be sure that the site you go to ends in *.gov*, not *.com*. HUD may refer you to a private broker's site later, which is okay.

Once you're on the official HUD site, you'll see a place that says, "Information by State." Enter your state and you'll be directed to the external site of a HUD-approved broker and given a list of available HUD properties. How many will you find? It depends very much on the market. In a booming market, very few of these properties will appear. In a down economy, when foreclosures are rampant, you'll find dozens. Remember that you must deal with HUD through one of its approved brokers. Like nearly all sellers, HUD pays the broker's fee. Locate a HUD broker in your community and let him or her know what you're looking for. A broker will be aware of all new listings, and working with one is a lot easier than monitoring the government Web site.

VA Foreclosures

VA foreclosures are handled differently. The Veterans Administration has contracted with Ocwen Loan Servicing LLC, West Palm Beach, Florida. Ocwen has a comprehensive Web site of all VA foreclosures at www.ocwen.com. (If the name Ocwen sounds strange to you, just read it backward. It stands for New Company. Now you know.) Click on its "Properties for Sale" button and again on the "VA Properties" button. Again, the number of properties listed will be small in a booming market but substantial in a market with high numbers of foreclosures. If you're interested in a property, call the local broker whose name and number are listed on the site.

The government also operates a Web site that combines homes for sale by HUD, the VA, and the USDA (Department of Agriculture). It's at *www.homesales.gov*.

Sheriff's Sales

First let's clarify our terminology here. If a borrower defaults on a loan, the trustee (the entity, such as a title company or escrow company that holds the title in trust until the loan is paid off) publishes a notice of default and eventually arranges for the property to be auctioned "on the courthouse steps." In about half the states, these are called "sheriff's sales," presumably because law enforcement is involved. As we told you in the previous chapter, when these properties are auctioned, there is frequently an upset bid period, usually 10 days, in which your bid can be upset by a bid that is at least 10 percent higher than your bid. In other words, your bid is not final at the auction and is not accepted until the upset period has passed.

Another type of "sheriff's sale" is one in which the sheriff sells properties that have been confiscated from criminals. These sales typically are final, and the funds go to the sheriff's office.

Sheriff's sales can also occur when the holders of mechanic's liens or other types of monetary judgments demand that the property be sold to recover money owed. These types of sales are extremely risky because all the successful bidder is getting is the interest the lien holder has in the property. If there are first, second, or third mortgages on the property, the successful bidder must assume these and keep them current if he or she wants to retain ownership in the property. Even then, the original owner may still be able to redeem the property.

There are myths about sheriff's sales that are compounded by movies like *House of Sea and Fog*, where Kathy, played by Jennifer Connelly, ignores a bill for a business license. The problem compounds over months until her home is sold at a sheriff's sale and picked up for a song by Bherani, a Persian immigrant played by Ben Kingsley.

It's good drama, but it rarely happens. When it does, the courts can quickly reverse the damage. The former owner will probably have several months (depending on the applicable state law) to repay the successful bidder with interest and redeem the property.

GSA Property Sales

When the federal government has surplus property, it turns to the General Services Administration (GSA) for help. There is an Office of Property Disposal that is part of the Public Building Service (PBS). Its Web site for real estate is at *http://www.pueblo.gsa.gov/cic_text/-fed_prog/realprop/realprop.htm*.

There you will find an astonishing array of real estate that is owned by the federal government and is being sold by bid. Each property gives you the e-mail address of the person who can send you an IFB (invitation for bid). As with any auction, you must be cautious. Don't bid sight unseen, however good a deal something seems to be.

Tax Lien Sales

If a property owner fails to pay his or her property taxes, the county will eventually attempt to collect the money owed it through a tax lien sale. It's very important to understand that if you successfully bid on a tax lien, you are not buying the property. What you're doing is lending the property owner the tax money owed; in return, you get a lien on the property that is in first position, ahead of mortgages, deeds of trust, and judgments. It is subordinate only to state tax liens. Where does that get you? The terms of the sale will vary widely from county to county, but if the amount you advanced is not repaid (plus an interest rate determined at the time of sale), you will one day be able to foreclose on the property. Since you'll be in first position at the sale on the courthouse steps, you have an excellent chance of acquiring the property. The worst that can happen is that a junior lien holder (probably the lender on the first mortgage) will step up and outbid you. If this happens, you will still get all of your money back with interest.

A tax deed sale is different. This is the sale of property that has already been foreclosed upon for back taxes and is now owned by the county. Here your successful bid will get you title to the property, free and clear of any liens, mortgages, and deeds of trust. If you get involved in this, be sure that you understand whether you're getting a deed or simply buying a lien.

Conclusion

There are some good buys to be had by buying property from the government. You don't need to pay a service to research these for you. All the information is available these days on government Web sites. You just need to know where to look. We include them in this chapter primarily for the purpose of making you aware of their existence. Unfortunately, the manner in which these properties are sold leaves little room for negotiating.

Key Points to Remember from This Chapter

- Government loan guarantees that enable people with marginal credit and minimal cash to buy homes often lead to foreclosures and good buys for investors.
- There are several different types of "sheriff's sales" that may result in some good buys, but these need to be approached with caution, as many problems can arise with these sales.

- Tax liens on properties sold at auction do not convey ownership and can be redeemed later by the property owners. To get ownership, the holder of the tax lien must foreclose on the property.
- Tax deeds do convey ownership because the property has already been through foreclosure and is owned by the county that is selling the property.
- Be very wary of seminar leaders selling what appear to be ways to get rich quick with government properties.
- Nearly all the information needed to purchase government-owned properties is available online and can be accessed from your home computer. Just be sure you are on the government sites that end in *.gov* and not commercial sites ending in *.com*.

7

How to Locate Owners of Property

In this chapter, we're going to spend some time discussing a topic that new investors find to be a serious challenge: how to locate sellers of property. Obviously you can't negotiate with the sellers unless you can find them. If you have followed the advice we gave you in our earlier books, you have found an area where the homes would make excellent rental properties. The prices are reasonable, and the homes, while modest, are presentable. On one street, you find the perfect opportunity. It's a nice house, but it clearly needs some loving care. The lawn is overgrown, the windows are dirty, and there is a string of Christmas tree lights along the eaves, even though it's June. Peering through the windows, you can see that the house is unoccupied because there is no furniture. This is what investors call "a diamond in the rough." How do you locate the owner? Here are some suggestions.

Talk to the Neighbors

This is our favorite method of finding investment opportunities. You'll be amazed at how much the neighbors know about the people on the street and how willing they are to share their information. "That belongs to Jenny Simpson," they'll tell you. "She went through a divorce and moved to a condo on Paradise Island with her boyfriend. She rented the place for a while, but the tenant got arrested for growing pot, and the place has been going downhill ever since."

The big advantage of talking to the neighbors is that you learn not only who owns the property, but also a lot about that person's financial situation and what might motivate him or her to give you a good buy. Also you'll learn if the person needs cash or would prefer an income stream. And even more important, you will learn about problems with the property or the neighborhood that the sellers may not want you to know.

If You Don't Know the Address

With tract homes, you can usually figure out the address, even if it's not on the house, the curb, or the mailbox. Just look at the sequence of numbers on each side of the house and figure it out. Odd numbers are usually on one side of the street and even numbers on the other. There may be a pattern to this in your state. In California, odd numbers are nearly always on the north side of an east-west road and the west side of a north-south road.

If you're in a nonconforming area, it becomes more difficult. In rural areas, there may not be a street number, only a mailbox address such as Rural Route 2 Box 12. Roger ran into this problem recently when trying to locate the owner of a property next to his golf club. He knew where the property was located (next to one of the greens), but he had no idea how to drive to the property or even what street it was on.

How to Locate Owners of Property

That's when the Web site *www.zillow.com* becomes invaluable. It contains an incredible amount of information about real estate and is free to use. This is a remarkable Web site that you should get to know. The folks at Zillow have obtained aerial pictures of the entire country and matched them to assessor's records that show the age and size of properties.

Here's how Roger located the address of the golf course property. First he went to *www.maps.google.com*. He typed in the name of the town, La Habra Heights, California, and clicked on "Search Maps." He centered the map on the golf course and started zooming in. He had to zoom in several times before the names of the lanes around the course started to appear. No lanes appeared to be very close to the course, but the nearest one appeared to be Green View Road. Then he went to the *www.zillow.com* Web site and typed Green View Road, La Habra Heights, California, into the Find Homes box. An aerial map appeared (similar to Google Earth), but it covered an area of at least five miles square.

Navigating this aerial map is like piloting a helicopter over the terrain, and like flying a helicopter, it takes some skill. Once Roger was in the correct location, he clicked on the property and a box appeared showing the street address; that the building had four bedrooms, three baths, and 3,086 square feet; and Zillow's estimate of its worth. (Zillow's estimates are informative but seem to be based on the average price for the neighborhood adjusted for the square footage of the house. They don't seem to adjust for the myriad of other factors that an appraiser would use. Try looking up a property that you own to see how accurate it is.) Clicking on the address in the box took him to a remarkably good aerial picture of the house. Zillow is an exceptional Web site that will keep you fascinated for hours. It is very popular, especially if you're in an urban area where data are readily available. At the time of this writing, it had received over 232 million hits.

You Know the Address, but Not the Name of the Owner

Here's where the county appraiser's Web sites will be invaluable. Go to *www.google.com* or a similar search engine and enter your county name followed by your state and the word *appraiser, assessor,* or *county recorder*. For example:

- Los Angeles County CA appraiser
- Buncombe County NC assessor
- Clarke County NV county recorder

You need to try all three titles because different counties use different ones.

Look for a Web site that has *.gov* as a suffix. There are hundreds of appraisers' and real estate brokers' Web sites that try to look like the official one, but they will all end in *.com*. You'll probably get a picture of your friendly county appraiser. He's the one responsible for assigning the tax valuation to your properties, and that is what the county uses to calculate your property taxes.

Some assessors' Web sites will provide owners' names and addresses; others won't, but will tell you how to find them. The Los Angeles assessor's site contains this notice:

The Assessor's office does not provide owner name information on their website. However, you may visit one of the Assessor's offices and obtain this information. Please go to Office Locations for the addresses and telephone numbers of the Assessor's central and district public service counters. Alternatively, you may request owner information for a specific property by filling out a Public Inquiry Form or e-mailing the Assessor's Public Correspondence Unit at helpdesk@assessor.lacounty.gov. Be sure to provide the Assessor's Identification Number and/or complete address of the property about which you are inquiring.

If you would like additional information regarding this subject, you may submit your question to our public service staff by using our Public Inquiry Form.

Since your taxes pay for government services such as this, you shouldn't hesitate to use them. Mike recently sent his two sons to the Buncombe County, North Carolina, courthouse with instructions to visit the Register of Deeds office, the Tax Assessor's office, and the Tax Collector's office. They were both surprised by how friendly and helpful the staff members in each office were.

Search for Local Information Sites

Look on a search engine such as Google for local community search engines. Take a look at *www.dallascad.org* to see how you can get the address, owner, and value of any property in Dallas. You can search by owner name, appraisal account number, and street address or by clicking on a map.

Title Companies

If you are lucky enough to live in a state where title companies will deal directly with consumers, property information is easy to get. How you buy title insurance varies widely from state to state and even within states. In North Carolina, where Mike lives, attorneys provide the title service as part of their real estate closing services and then obtain the insurance from title companies. In southern California, where Roger lives, escrow companies specialize in closing real estate deals and get insurance from title companies. In northern California, title companies handle real estate closings themselves. The best thing to do is ask your friendly real estate agent how closings are handled in your area. You'll probably find that title companies offer free search services to real estate agents because they want to attract their business. If that's the case, you can request all the information you need on properties by having your agent get a complimentary preliminary title report for you. All you'll need is the street address or the assessor's parcel number.

Real Estate Agents

Many investors believe that they have to find properties that are For Sale By Owner (FSBO) in order to find deals. Nothing could be further from the truth. Real estate agents are an excellent source for finding properties. Remember that we are talking about finding owners, and that's different from negotiating deals. Real estate agents network with one another; they have access to Multiple Listing Services and other sources of information about properties for sale. These people earn their living selling real estate, so why would anyone be reluctant to use them to locate the owners of properties for sale?

One caution about working with real estate agents is that once you have identified a prospective property, you want to be sure you know for whom the agent is working. Unless you have a written agreement stating that the agent is working for you as a buyer's agent, you can bet that the agent's fiduciary duty is to the seller; therefore, you want to be careful about how much information you divulge to this representative of the seller.

Throughout the 1990s, Mike worked almost exclusively with one agent who represented him in all his transactions. They had a written agreement that the agent's loyalty in all transactions involving Mike would be to him and not to the sellers. Although Mike's agent made the other listing agents fully aware of this arrangement, he was able to obtain information that he would not have had access to without his agent's involvement. With this agent's assistance, he purchased dozens of rental units worth several million dollars.

Mike had one transaction in particular that provided a good example of how a buyer's agent can be a big asset in the purchase negotiation. As described in Chapter 27 of our book *The Weekend Millionaire's Secrets to Investing in Real Estate*, this agent found a commercial property that he felt would be a good addition to Mike's portfolio. The seller was asking $242,000 for the property, which had an assessed value of $243,100. Although the property was not in the best area, Mike's agent said that the property had been on the market for quite some time, and he felt the seller might be flexible and possibly even provide part of the financing in order to facilitate a sale.

Mike and his agent inspected the property, which had formerly been a small textile manufacturing business located between two much larger operations. Because of problems with the area, Mike told his agent that he wouldn't want to pay more than about $150,000 for the property. After conferring with the seller's agent, Mike's agent learned a number of things that enabled him to negotiate a successful purchase.

He learned that the owner had tried to sell the business before he retired, but had been unable to do so. He learned that the owner had closed the business and was now trying to sell the building to provide additional income for his retirement. He also learned that there was a small mortgage on the property that would have to be paid off at closing, but that the owner would be willing to finance the purchase as long as he could get enough cash at closing to pay the mortgage and real estate commission. Probably the most valuable information Mike's agent learned was that the seller would be flexible on the price, but that he had made a promise to his wife that he would not sell for less than $200,000. Because Mike's agent was a fellow real estate agent, he was able to obtain all of this valuable information from the seller's agent, who would probably not have shared it directly with Mike.

Armed with the information his agent had obtained, Mike negotiated back and forth with the seller until they agreed upon a purchase offer of $200,000 that required $60,000 cash at closing, with the seller agreeing to take back a purchase money note for $140,000, payable at $1,000 per month for 140 months. He also agreed to subordinate his note to a senior encumbrance.

Let's examine this transaction to see how the information Mike's agent obtained helped make a successful negotiation possible. First, it was important for Mike to know that the seller was retired and had been trying to sell the property for several months. Second, knowing that there was a mortgage on the property told Mike that although the seller was retired, he still had to make a mortgage payment each month. If they could strike a deal, the seller would benefit in two ways: the cash he was paying out each month would stop, and in its place he would start receiving income in the form of the payments he would receive from Mike. The seller's cash flow would improve by the combined total of the two payments.

As unlikely as it may seem, the most important information Mike received was the fact that the seller had promised his wife not to sell for less than $200,000. By taking back a note for $140,000 payable at $1,000 per month for 140 months at 0 percent interest, the seller was able to show his wife a contract for $200,000, and Mike was able to keep his cash flow about the same as it would have been if he had paid $150,000 for the property and borrowed the full amount from a bank at the then going rate of 8 percent.

These tidbits of information that a buyer's agent can obtain are often difficult for an individual to get. As we've said throughout this book, information is power in a negotiation. Never discount real estate agents as great sources of both locating properties and gathering information.

Key Points to Remember from This Chapter

- Neighbors can be a great source of information.
- There is a world of information available on the Internet.
- Public records available at county courthouses contain a tremendous amount of information on individual properties and owners. In most areas, this information is accessible online on the county's Web site.
- In states where title companies will deal directly with individuals, they will often provide preliminary title searches and more at no charge.

How to Locate Owners of Property

- Don't overlook real estate agents as excellent sources of properties for sale. Although most agents work for the sellers, they still have a vested interest in helping you put deals together.
- Buyer's agents are often able to get information about a seller that you as an individual cannot get.

8

Negotiations with Real Estate Agents

As your real estate portfolio grows, you will find yourself dealing more and more with real estate agents. The relationships that you build with them can make or break you as an investor.

First, let's examine the fiduciary relationship of the parties when a broker is involved (*fiduciary* means "trust"). The owner of a property hires a real estate broker to list that property for sale. This is an employment contract wherein the owner hires the broker to use due diligence (that means "care and attention") to find a buyer who is ready, willing, and able to purchase the property. It's important to understand that this is an employment contract because a situation may occur in which the sellers have accepted an offer and then want to change their minds about selling. Are they contractually obligated to sell? The answer is, no, they are not, but they are obligated to pay the broker because the broker did her job when she delivered a buyer who was ready, willing, and able to buy at an agreed-upon price. (If the seller accepts the buyer's offer, it then becomes a contract between the buyer and the seller. If the seller then refuses to close, the buyer could file a lawsuit demanding specific performance under this contract, but this rarely happens.)

The relationship between buyers, sellers, real estate agents, and real estate brokers can be confusing at times, so we'll try to clarify it. Real estate agents cannot contract directly with buyers or sellers. They must work as subagents of their broker. Any commission money flows from the principals (buyers or sellers) to the brokers, who then pay the agents.

The agent who represents the buyer is called the *selling agent*, because he or she is the one responsible for making the sale to a buyer. Technically, the selling agent is a subagent of the selling broker and the selling broker is a subagent of the listing broker, as is the listing agent. We've always found this a bit confusing, and you will too until you understand that all these people are in fact working for the seller. It is the seller who is paying everyone. It is critical that you understand this relationship when you are trying to negotiate a purchase.

Unless you contract with a buyer's agent to represent you as the buyer, you should never say to a selling agent something like, "Take them an offer for $200,000, but if they won't accept that, I'm willing to go to $220,000." You must understand that most agents are working for the seller and would have a fiduciary duty to share that information with the seller. Also, that agent would not be allowed to tell you anything that might be detrimental to the seller's interests. That would include telling you that the seller was under pressure to sell, letting you know that a property down the street sold for less, or revealing any concessions that the seller might be willing to make.

Buyer's Agents

A true buyer's agent works only for the buyer and is paid by the buyer. Although there are not many of them out there, you may be able to find a buyer's agent who will represent you. If so, you will be asked to sign an agreement, much like a listing agreement, that spells out that the agent has a fiduciary duty to you, not to the sellers. Buyer's agents often require you to pay them a retainer fee and then a percentage of the purchase price. While this may seem like a great plan for real estate investors, it has never caught on. One of the few places you will find it is in commercial real estate, where large chain corporations hire buyer's agents to locate sites in multiple markets.

Buyer's Agency

You may run into agents who say they are buyer's agents, but they are not unless they are hired solely by the buyer. As long as the sellers still pay them through shared commissions, they are not buyer's agents. The concept of a buyer's agency came about because the traditional way of listing and selling real estate was opening up brokers to lawsuits. Think about it: all the agents were working for the seller, which meant that they were not able to say anything to the buyer that would be detrimental to or weaken the position of the seller. For many years, buyers didn't know this. They thought their agent was working for them. The brokers were getting caught in the legal crossfire, with the sellers saying, "You shouldn't have told the buyer what you did!" and the buyers saying, "You should have told us, but you didn't!" Lawyers for the brokers realized that they would be less likely to get sued if the listing brokers and their subagents declared that their loyalty was to the seller alone and the selling brokers and their agents declared that their loyalty was to the buyer, even though they would share in the commissions paid by the sellers. That concept is now spreading across the country. Until you know whether an agent represents you or the sellers, be careful how much of your negotiating strategy you share with that agent.

Back before buyer's agents began to gain acceptance in the marketplace, Mike convinced a real estate broker friend of his to become his buyer's broker. They drafted an agreement between them that required the broker to notify selling brokers that he represented Mike alone. The arrangement worked out very well because Mike's broker was able to get information that the selling brokers would not have shared had Mike been dealing with them directly. This enabled Mike to structure dozens of offers that met the seller's unique needs and resulted in the purchase of many properties over a number of years. By gathering information about the sellers, Mike's buyer's broker not only facilitated the sale of the properties, but made a nice fee each time Mike purchased one.

Who Is the Agent Working For?

There's a legal way of explaining the answer to that, and there's also a practical way. After all the years we have spent in the real estate business, we both agree on the answer: *Agents are not working primarily for the buyer or for the seller. They are working for themselves.* Their goal is to get the deal put together as quickly and as simply as they can in order to earn a commission.

As a real estate broker, Roger was involved in dozens of hard-to-close deals where either the buyer or the seller had to compromise to put the deal together. He came to the conclusion that it was easier for him to get the buyers to budge than to get the sellers to do so. If the buyers went up on their price, it might mean that they would have to make a slightly higher down payment and their monthly payments might go up by a few dollars, but it also meant that he would earn a higher commission. If the sellers came down on their price, it meant a reduction in his commission and took cold hard cash out of the seller's pocket.

Finding an Agent Who Will Work with Investors

Some agents love to work with investors, and some agents hate it. The plus side is that if the agent can find an investor who is interested in acquiring a string of properties, the agent can develop a constant source of income. What could be better for an agent than having a ready, willing, and able buyer if he or she can find the right properties? The agent can be on the lookout for properties that meet the investor's requirements and close deals quickly. The downside is that investors are not interested in buying properties at retail prices. To make the numbers work, we must buy at wholesale values, which means presenting low-priced offers or ones asking for favorable financing from the sellers. Based on the conventional fiduciary duty to sellers, many brokers and agents find this difficult to do.

Agents who are good at presenting wholesale offers have a distinct personality profile and like to do it. They are very assertive and very unemotional. Assertive means that they are take-charge people. They are the "If anybody is running this thing, I want it to be me!" people of the world. Another characteristic of assertive people is that they have a strong desire to persuade people to come around to their point of view. They are always trying to convince people to live in their part of town and drive the kind of car they drive. The unemotional part of their personality means that they don't need to be liked to get things done. Their drive is to get the deal closed, not necessarily to make friends with the sellers.

How do you find an agent like this? Someone who is assertive, unemotional, and wants to work with investors? You have to interview a lot of agents to find ones that click. If they are assertive, they will approach you with their hand out and a friendly greeting. They will quickly size up the car you drive and how much you paid for your wristwatch and shoes. Shoes are important because a rich person might wear jeans and a T-shirt but will often wear expensive shoes. Their approach is, "Let me know what you're looking for, and I'll go find it for you," not, "Let's get to know each other." Be sure to level with your agent. The more your agent knows about you, the better job that he or she will be able to do without wasting any time. If you don't have much cash or have credit problems, the agent needs to know that so that he or she doesn't spend time on deals that would require cash and good credit.

Don't Agents Buy All the Good Deals?

Not as often as you'd think, for a couple of reasons. Some agents think that it's unethical to snap up the good buys when they should be serving their clients and customers by offering the good deals to them. (In the world of real estate, a seller is a client and a buyer is a customer.) A bigger reason is that most agents need the cash flow that comes from closing deals for their buyers and sellers. They simply can't afford to buy every good deal that comes along and still eat.

Should an Investor Get a Real Estate License?

This is one of the few areas where Mike and Roger disagree. Roger has been a California broker for almost 30 years and thinks that being in the industry is a big advantage. You get to know the market well, and you can spot good buys quickly. Mike thinks that having a real estate license subjects you to undesirable scrutiny and a potential liability that does not exist for unlicensed buyers. Having a real estate license means that you are considered a professional in the eyes of the law and are treated differently from the way you would be if you were not licensed.

You must consider a few key points before you decide. (1) If you are an agent (not a broker) and you put your license with a broker so that you can list and sell real estate, you will have to pay your broker a cut when you buy and sell for your own portfolio. The plus side is that you earn commissions on your own purchases, which can offset the down payment that you must make when you buy. (2) If you have a real estate license, you have a fiduciary relationship with your buyers and sellers. You must declare that you are licensed when you offer to buy or sell. Include this expression in your purchase offers to protect yourself from lawsuits: "Buyer is a licensed real estate agent (or broker) buying below market value for investment purposes and will be receiving part of the sales commission." (3) If you call a For Sale By Owner, the seller will probably ask you if you're a real estate agent. If you are, he or she may not want to talk to you, assuming that you're only trying to list the property.

Will Agents Cut Their Commission to Put a Deal Together?

They hate to do it, but broker's fees have become a lot more negotiable since the last run-up in prices. Although real estate commissions have always been a matter of negotiation between the seller and the listing broker, it used to be almost the rule that the listing broker would charge 6 percent of the selling price and split that 50/50 with the selling broker. Then real estate prices doubled and 6 percent of a $500,000 listing became $30,000. That's a lot of money. With that kind of money on the table, agents have become a lot more willing to negotiate their commission.

The other thing that is becoming more common is for agents to be willing to accept all or part of their commission in the form of a promissory note so that the buyers can close with less cash out of their pocket. Agents can build a portfolio of interest-bearing notes from transactions where they have done this and provide themselves with a stream of steady income.

Negotiating Strategy for Dealing with Agents

Accept the fact that agents hate to let buyers meet their sellers. If a selling agent is showing a property to a buyer, that agent would rather the seller not be there. It avoids the bad feelings when the buyer looks at the seller's home and says things like, "We could make this really nice."

You, as a buyer, would love to sit down with the seller and convince him that he should sell to you. The agent doesn't want to let you do that. What we suggest is that you challenge the agent by saying, "Go ahead and present the offer to the seller, but if you can't get him to accept it, I'd like to reserve the right to meet with the seller myself."

This challenges the agent to get the offer accepted and greatly improves your chances.

Key Points to Remember from This Chapter

- A listing is an employment contract. It doesn't obligate the seller to sell.
- There is no contract for sale until an offer with an earnest money deposit is signed by a buyer and accepted in writing by a seller, and the acceptance is communicated to the buyer.
- Only brokers can accept money in exchange for facilitating the sale of real estate. Agents are subagents of a broker.
- Traditionally, all agents are working for the seller because that's who usually pays them.
- A buyer's agency is one that by agreement works solely for the buyer.
- In the practical world, agents work primarily for themselves, not for the buyers or the sellers.
- When seeking a buyer's agent, look for an assertive, unemotional agent who loves working with investors.
- Agents can't afford to buy up all the good deals.
- There are pros and cons to being licensed.
- Agents frequently negotiate their fees to make a deal work.
- Challenge the agent to get offers accepted and let him or her know that you have other options if he or she can't do so.

9

Beginning Negotiating Gambits

A gambit is a chess term that means any maneuver to gain an advantage. Players use beginning gambits to get the game started, middle gambits to keep up the momentum, and ending gambits when they are getting ready to checkmate the other player—or, in business parlance, when they are putting the deal together. Chess players who are purists will argue that the word *gambit* involves the willingness to take a risk and lose a piece, so it applies only to the opening moves, when pawns may be sacrificed. In negotiating, we use the broader sense of beginning, middle, and ending gambits. In this chapter, we'll teach you the gambits that you use in the early stages of the negotiation to be sure that you're setting it up for a successful conclusion.

Never Say Yes to the First Offer

The reason that you should never say yes to the first offer (or counteroffer) is that it automatically triggers two thoughts in the seller's mind.

Let's say that you're thinking of buying a small house in your neighborhood that would make a great rental. The owners are trying to sell it themselves, and they're asking $100,000. That is such a terrific price for the perfect rental house that you can't wait to get down there and snap it up before somebody else beats you to it. On the way there, however, you start thinking that it would be a mistake to offer them what they're asking, so you decide to make a super low offer of $90,000 just to judge the sellers' reaction. You show up at their house, look the house over, and say to the owners, "It's not what I'm looking for, but I'll give you $90,000."

You're waiting for them to explode with rage at such a low offer, but what actually happens is that the husband looks at the wife and says, "What do you think, dear?"

The wife says, "Let's go ahead and get rid of it."

Does this exchange make you jump for joy? Does it leave you thinking, "Wow, I can't believe what a deal I got! I couldn't have gotten it for a penny less"?

We don't think so. We believe you're probably thinking

1. I could have done better.
2. Something must be wrong with it.

If your son came to you and said, "May I borrow the car tonight?" and you said, "Sure, son, take it. Have a wonderful time," wouldn't he automatically think, "I could have done better. I could have gotten $20 for the movie as well"? And wouldn't he automatically think, "What's going on here? Why do they want me out of the house? What's going on that I don't understand?"

This is a very easy negotiating principle to understand, but it's a very hard one to remember when you're in the thick of a tense negotiation. You may have formed a mental picture of how you expect the seller to respond to your offer, and that's a dangerous thing to do. Napoleon Bonaparte once said, "The unforgivable sin of a commander is to 'form a picture'—to assume that the enemy will act a certain way in a given situation, when in fact his response may be altogether different."

Many years ago, Roger bought 100 acres of land in Eatonville, Washington, a beautiful little town just west of Mount Rainier. The seller was asking $185,000 for the land.

Before we continue with this story, let's make it clear that we don't recommend buying land as an investment. It's more of a speculation than an investment. You're better off investing in rental properties for many reasons:

- Banks don't like to lend on vacant land, so financing is frequently provided by the seller, and often at a higher percentage rate than a bank would charge.
- Unless you're buying junk land from a developer, you won't be able to borrow the 80 or 90 percent that you would be able to on a house.
- Land doesn't generate any income.
- When you sell land, you will probably have to carry back financing.
- You cannot depreciate land for tax purposes.

However, Roger analyzed the property and decided that if he could get it for $150,000, it would be a terrific buy and would give him the opportunity to sell it and make a good profit. He bracketed that price and asked the real estate agent to present an offer to the seller at $115,050. (Specific numbers build credibility. You're more likely to get an offer like this accepted than to get a counter to it.)

He went back to his home in La Habra Heights, California, leaving the agent to present the offer to the seller. He thought he'd be lucky if he got any kind of counteroffer on such a low proposal. To his amazement, he got the offer back in the mail a few days later, accepted at the price and on the terms that he had proposed. He knew that he had gotten a terrific buy on the land. Within a year, he'd sold 60 of the acres for more than he'd paid for the whole hundred. Later he sold another 20 acres for more than he'd paid for the whole hundred. So when the sellers accepted his offer, he should have been thinking, "Wow, that's terrific. I couldn't have gotten a lower price." That's what he should have been thinking, but he wasn't. To this day, he is still thinking, "I could have done better." This feeling doesn't have anything to do with the price—it has to do only with the way the other person reacts to the proposal.

The second thought Roger had was, "Wow, I'm going to take a good look at the preliminary title report when it comes in, because something is going on here that I don't understand. If they are willing to accept an offer that I didn't think would even get a counter, something must be wrong."

What is a preliminary title report? When a seller accepts your offer, you should take the signed agreement and the deposit check to the entity that will handle the title transfer. Depending on your state, this will be an escrow company that specializes in real estate transactions, a title company, or an attorney. To protect yourself, you should always buy title insurance. This is an insurance policy that guarantees that the seller owns the property and has transferred good title to you. Either your escrow officer will order a preliminary title report from the title insurance company or your attorney will research the public records and give you a title opinion. Your offer should always be contingent upon your approval of the "prelim," as it is called, because some interesting things can show up that affect the value of the property.

- You'll see who the owner of record is and how title to the property is held.

- You'll see a list of encumbrances on the property, which could include loans that the seller owes, taxes that are due, and liens and/or judgments against the seller.
- You'll see a list of easements. While the concept of ownership is that you own the property from the center of the earth to the heavens, you may find that someone else owns the mineral rights under the property. You'll probably find that utility companies have rights of way allowing them to string wires over your property.
- You may find a Lis Pedens. This is an attorney's way of warning you that the property is involved in a pending lawsuit.

In your offers, you should ask the seller to give you a General Warranty Deed at closing, and even then you will want to obtain title insurance to guarantee that you got what you thought you were getting.

You may also find that there are conditions on the title. Here's where things get interesting. Anyone who has owned the property in the past can put a condition on the title. It could be a homeowner's association that has a prohibition on your changing the oil in your car in the driveway or one that stops you from painting your front door bright red. Some associations may even prohibit you from renting the property.

Some conditions can substantially affect the value of a property. Roger remembers researching a property next to a freeway in San Dimas, California, that would have made a great strip shopping center. When he researched the title, however, he found that a former owner had prohibited the sale of alcohol on the premises. That meant that there could not be a liquor store in the shopping center. A liquor store is a great traffic builder, and if it is leased on a percentage lease (where the landlord gets a percentage of the sales), it can be a great moneymaker. A condition like that dramatically affects the value of the property. You should always inspect the preliminary title report carefully.

> ### Key Points to Remember
>
> - Never say yes to the first offer or counteroffer from the other side. It automatically triggers two thoughts: I could have done better (and next time I will), and something must be wrong.
> - The biggest danger comes when you have formed a mental picture of how the seller will respond to your proposal and he or she comes back with a response that is far different from what you expected. Prepare for this possibility so that it won't catch you off guard.

Ask for More than You Expect to Get

One of the cardinal rules of negotiating is that you should ask the other side for more than you expect to get. Henry Kissinger (Richard Nixon's secretary of state) went so far as to say, "Effectiveness at the bargaining table depends upon your ability to overstate your initial demands." Think of some reasons why you should do this:

- Why should you ask the seller to give you a lower price than you think you have a chance of getting?
- Why should you ask the seller to carry back financing at 0 percent even though you don't think for a moment that he or she will do that?
- Why should your offer include the seller's paying for closing costs, title insurance, and attorney's fees?
- Why should your offer include items of personal property such as appliances, curtains, area rugs, and so on?

If you thought about this, you probably came up with a few good reasons for asking for more than you expect to get. The obvious answer is that it gives you some negotiating room. If you're buying, you can always go up, but you can never come down. (When we get to ending negotiating gambits, we'll show you how to Nibble for more. Some things *are* easier to get at the end of the negotiation than they are at the beginning.) What you should be asking for is your MPP—your maximum plausible position. This is the most that you can ask for and still have the other side see some plausibility in your position.

The less you know about the other side, the more extreme your initial position should be, for two reasons:

1. You may be off in your assumptions. If you don't know the seller or his or her needs well, he or she may be willing to take far less than you think.
2. With a seller you haven't met, you will appear much more cooperative if you're able to make larger concessions. The fastest way to build rapport (not the best way, but the fastest) is to be able to make concessions to the other side. The better you know the other person and his or her needs, the more you can modify your position. Conversely, if the sellers don't know you yet, their initial demands may be more than they will be willing to accept once they get to know you better.

If you're asking for far more than your maximum plausible position, imply some flexibility. If your initial position seems outrageous to the other person and your attitude is "take it or leave it," you may not even get the negotiations started. The other person's response may simply be, "Then we don't have anything to talk about." You can get away with an outrageous opening position if you imply some flexibility.

If you're buying real estate directly from the seller, you might say, "I realize that you're asking $200,000 for the property, and based on everything you know, that may seem like a fair price to you. Perhaps you know something that I don't, but based on all the research that I've done, it seems to me that we should be talking about something closer to $160,000." At that, the seller may be thinking, "That's ridiculous. I'll never let it go for that, but he does seem to be sincere. What do I have to lose if I spend some time negotiating with him, just to see how high I can get him to go?"

Unless you're already an experienced negotiator, here's the problem you will have with this. Your real MPP is probably much lower than you think it is. Most of us fear being ridiculed by other people, and so we're reluctant to take a position that will cause another person to laugh at us or put us down. Because of this intimidation, you will probably feel like modifying your MPP to the point where your initial offer is more than the minimum amount that the seller would think is plausible.

Another reason for asking for more than you expect to get will be obvious to you if you're a positive thinker: you just might get it. You don't know how the universe is aligned that day. Perhaps your patron saint is leaning over a cloud looking down at you and thinking, "Wow, look at that nice investor. She's been working so hard for so long now, let's just give her a break." You might just get what you ask for, and the only way you'll find out is to ask for it.

Another advantage of asking for more than you expect to get is that it prevents the negotiation from deadlocking when you're dealing with an egotistical person. All we mean by that is a seller who is proud of his or her ability to negotiate. You've met these people, haven't you? They are horse traders from way back. They're convinced that they can have a win with you in the negotiations, and if you don't give them room to have a win, the negotiations will deadlock on you.

A final reason—and it's the reason why we say that you should ask for more than you expect to get—is that this is the only way in which you can create a climate that allows the other person to feel that he or she won. If you go in with your best offer up front, there's no way that you can negotiate with the people on the other side and leave them feeling that they won.

- Inexperienced investors typically want to start with their best offer.
- They also tend to think, "If I don't make a reasonable offer, the sellers will laugh at me."

Beginning Negotiating Gambits

Know the value of asking for more than you expect to get. With real estate, price is only one part of value; payment terms is the other. If you're not comfortable offering a very low price, try offering full price and ask the seller to finance the purchase at very low or even 0 percent interest. What you want to do is create a climate in which you can make concessions that will allow the seller to feel that he or she won.

In highly publicized negotiations, such as when football players or airline pilots go on strike, the initial demands that both sides make are outlandish. Roger remembers being involved in a union negotiation where the initial demands were unbelievably outrageous. The union's demand was to triple the employees' wages. The company's opening was to make the operation an open shop—in other words, a voluntary union that would effectively destroy the union's power at that location.

When Sudanese rebels took three Red Cross workers hostage, they demanded $100 million for their release. Fortunately, nobody took this seriously, and they quickly dropped their demand to $2.5 million. Congressman Bill Richardson, who would later ride his negotiating skills all the way to being our ambassador to the United Nations, governor of New Mexico, and a presidential candidate, sat under a tree ignoring the rebels, who were waving guns at him. He eventually secured their release for five tons of rice, four old jeeps, and some radios from Red Cross relief supplies.

Roger remembers being in Beijing, China, when the country first started admitting foreign visitors. He wanted a pedishaw ride to his hotel, which was only two blocks away (a pedishaw is like a rickshaw, but it has a bicycle on the front). When the other pedishaw drivers realized that he was an American, they went wild with delight. They all gathered around and advised the lucky driver how to handle the negotiations. One of them told him to ask Roger for $10, another said $20, and finally they agreed that $50 would be an appropriate place to start the negotiations. They didn't realize that Roger taught negotiating, so when he eventually agreed to give the driver $1, which was more than a day's wages, the driver was very happy.

Great negotiators know that the initial demands in these types of negotiations are always extreme, so they don't let this bother them.

Great negotiators also know that as the negotiations progress, the two sides will work their way toward the middle, where they will find a solution that both sides can accept. Then each side can call a press conference and announce that it won in the negotiations.

An attorney friend tested this theory for us. He was representing the buyer of a piece of real estate, and even though he had a good deal worked out, he thought, "I'll see how the rule of Asking for More than You Expect to Get works." He dreamt up 23 paragraphs of requests to make of the seller. Some of them were ridiculous. He felt sure that at least half of them would be thrown out right away. To his amazement, he found that the seller of the property took strong objection to only one of the sentences in one of the paragraphs.

Even then, the attorney, as we had taught him, didn't give in right away. He held out for a couple of days before he finally and reluctantly conceded the point. Although he had given away only one sentence in 23 paragraphs of requests, that concession allowed the seller to still feel that he had won in the negotiation.

Always leave some room to let the other person have a win. Great negotiators always ask for more than they expect to get.

Read this fable about asking for more and see how it projects some very solid folk wisdom. There was once a very old couple who lived in a dilapidated thatched hut on a remote Pacific island. One day a hurricane blew through the village and demolished their home. Because they were much too old and poor to rebuild the hut, the couple moved in with their daughter and her husband. This arrangement precipitated an unpleasant domestic situation, as the daughter's hut was barely big enough for her, her husband, and their four children, let alone the in-laws.

The daughter went to the wise person of the village, explained the problem, and asked, "Whatever will we do?"

The wise person puffed slowly on a pipe and then responded, "You have chickens, don't you?"

"Yes," she replied, "we have 10 chickens."

"Then bring the chickens into the hut with you."

This seemed ludicrous to the daughter, but she followed the wise person's advice. The move naturally exacerbated the problem, and the situation was soon unbearable, as feathers as well as hostile words flew around the hut. The daughter returned to the wise person, pleading again for advice.

"You have pigs, do you not?"

"Yes, we have three pigs."

"Then you must bring the pigs into your hut with you."

That seemed to be ridiculous advice, but to question the wise person was unthinkable, so she brought the pigs into the hut. Life was now truly unlivable, with 8 people, 10 chickens, and 3 pigs sharing one tiny, noisy hut.

The next day the daughter, fearing for her family's sanity, approached the wise person with a final desperate plea. "Please," she cried, "we can't live like this. Tell me what to do and I'll do it, but please help us."

This time the wise person's response was puzzling, but easier to follow. "Now remove the chickens and the pigs from your hut." She quickly evicted the animals, and the entire family lived happily together for the rest of their days. The moral of the story: a deal always looks better after something has been thrown out!

Ask for more than you expect to get. It seems like such an obvious principle, but it's something that you can count on in a negotiation. The more you ask for, the more you're going to get.

Key Points to Remember

- Ask for more than you expect to get for five reasons:
  1. You just might get it.
  2. It gives you some negotiating room.
  3. It raises the perceived value of what you're offering.
  4. It prevents the negotiation from deadlocking.
  5. It creates a climate in which the other side feels that it won.
- Your objective should be to advance your MPP—your maximum plausible position.
- If your initial proposal is extreme, imply some flexibility. This encourages the other side to negotiate with you.
- The less you know about the other side, the more extreme your position should be. A stranger is more likely to surprise you, and you can build goodwill by making bigger concessions.

Bracketing

The next question has to be, if you're asking for more than you expect to get, how much more than you expect to get should you ask for? The answer is that you should bracket your objective. Your initial proposal should be the same distance from your objective as the other side's proposal.

In simpler language, assume that you will end up midway between the two opening negotiating positions.

Of course, it's not always true that you'll end up in the middle, but that is a good assumption to make if you don't have anything else on which to base your opening position. Assume that you'll end up in the middle, midway between the two opening negotiating positions. If you track it, we think that the frequency with which this happens will amaze you, both in little things and in big things.

Your son comes to you and says that he needs $20 for a project he's working on. You say, "No way. I'm not going to give you $20. Do you realize that when I was your age, I got 50 cents a week allowance, and I had to work for that? I'll give you $10 and not a penny more."

Your son says, "I can't do it for $10, dad."

Now you have established the negotiating range. He's asking for $20. You're willing to pay $10. See how often you end up at $15. In our culture, splitting the difference seems fair.

So often, in little things and in big things, we end up splitting the difference. With bracketing, great negotiators are assured that if that happens, they still get what they want.

To bracket, you must get the other person to state his or her position first. If the other person can get you to state your position first, then that person can bracket you, so that, if you end up splitting the difference (as so often happens), she ends up getting what she wanted. That's an underlying principle of negotiating: get the other person to state his or her position first. It may not be as bad as you fear, and it's the only way you can bracket the proposal.

Another benefit of bracketing is that it tells you how big your concessions can be as the negotiation progresses. If the seller is asking $200,000 and you can make the deal work at $190,000, you should offer $180,000. If the seller comes down to $197,000, you can go up to $183,000 and still have your objective in the middle. If the seller comes down to $196,000, you can come up to $184,000.

There's a danger here, however. Your responses should not become so predictable that the other side can detect your pattern of concessions. We illustrated this with mathematically computed concessions to make the point clear, but you should vary your moves slightly so that the seller cannot detect a pattern.

Key Points to Remember

- Bracket the other side's proposal so that if you end up splitting the difference, you still get what you want.
- You can bracket only if you get the other person to state his or her position first.
- Continue bracketing as you zero in on your objective with concessions.

Flinch at Proposals

Great negotiators know that you should always Flinch—react to the other side's proposals with shock and surprise.

Let's say that you are in a resort area, and you stop to watch one of those charcoal sketch artists. He doesn't have his price posted. You ask him how much he charges, and he tells you $15. If that doesn't appear to shock you, his next words will be, "And $5 extra for color." If you still don't appear to be shocked, he will say, "And we have these shipping cartons here; you'll need one of these, too."

Perhaps you know someone who would never Flinch like that because it's beneath his or her dignity. People like this walk into a store and say to the clerk, "How much is the coat in the window?"

The clerk responds, "$2,000."

They say, "That's not bad!" Instead, they should be acting as though they're having a heart attack.

We know that it sounds dumb and it sounds ridiculous, but the truth of the matter is that when people make a proposal to you, they are watching for your reaction. They may not think for a moment that you'll go along with their request. They've just thrown it out to see what your reaction will be. For example:

- The seller asks $250,000 for the property when she'd be happy to get $220,000.

Beginning Negotiating Gambits

- The seller asks you for a $10,000 earnest money deposit.
- You're buying a house, and the seller wants to stay in the house for two weeks after the transaction closes.

In each of these situations, the other side may not have thought for a moment that you would go along with the request, but if you don't Flinch, he or she will automatically think, "Maybe I can get them to go along with that. I didn't think they would, but I think I'll be a tough negotiator and see how far I can get them to go."

It's very interesting to observe a negotiation when you know what both sides are thinking. Wouldn't that be fascinating for you? Wouldn't you love to know what's going on in the seller's mind when you're negotiating with him or her?

When Roger conducts his one- or two-day "Secrets of Power Negotiating" seminars, he breaks the attendees into groups to practice the principles that we teach. He breaks the audience up into buyers, sellers, and referees. The referees are in a very interesting position because they have been in on the planning sessions of both the buyers and the sellers. They know each side's negotiating range. They know what the buyers' opening offer is going to be, and they know how far each side will go. Say the sellers of the property would go as low as $700,000, but they start as high as $800,000. The buyers may start at $600,000, but they're prepared to go to $750,000 if they have to. So the negotiating range is $600,000 to $800,000, but the acceptance range is $700,000 to $750,000. The acceptance range embraces the price levels at which the buyers' and the sellers' negotiating ranges overlap. If they do overlap and there is an acceptance range, it's almost certain that the final price to which they agree will fall within this range.

Buyer's negotiating range	Acceptance range	Seller's negotiating range
$600K to $750K	$700K to $750K	$700K to $800K

If the top of the buyers' negotiating range is lower than the bottom of the sellers' negotiating range, then one or both sides will have to compromise their objectives.

The negotiation starts with each side trying to get the other side to put its offer on the table first. After a while, someone has to break the ice, so the sellers may suggest $800,000 (which is at the top of their negotiating range). They believe that this is ridiculously high, and they barely have the nerve to propose it. They think they're going to be laughed out of the room the minute they do. However, to their surprise, the buyers don't appear to be that shocked. The sellers expect the buyers to say, "You want us to do what? You must be out of your minds." What they actually respond with is much milder, perhaps, "We don't think we'd be prepared to go that high." In an instant, the negotiation has changed. A moment ago, $800,000 had seemed to be an impossible goal. Now the sellers are thinking that perhaps the two aren't as far apart as they had thought they were. Now they're thinking, "Let's hang in there. Let's be tough negotiators. Maybe we will get this much."

Flinching is critical because most people believe what they see more than they believe what they hear. The visual overrides the auditory in most people. It's safe for you to assume that at least 70 percent of the people with whom you negotiate will be visuals, for whom what they see is more important than what they hear. We're sure you've been exposed to some neurolinguistic programming. You know that people are either visual, auditory, or kinesthetic (what they feel is paramount). There are a few gustatory (taste) and olfactory (smell) people around, but not many, and they're usually chefs or perfume blenders.

If you'd like to know which type you are, close your eyes for 10 seconds and think of the house in which you lived when you were 10 years old. You probably saw the house in your mind; if so, you're a visual.

Perhaps you didn't get a good visual picture, but you heard what was going on, perhaps trains passing by or children playing. That means you're auditory. Auditories tend to be very auditory. Neil Berman is a psychotherapist friend of Roger's in Santa Fe, New Mexico. He can remember every conversation he's ever had with a patient, but if he meets one of his patients in the supermarket, he doesn't remember him or her. The minute the person says good morning to him, however, he thinks, "Oh yes, that's the bipolar personality with antisocial tendencies."

The third possibility is that you didn't so much see the house or hear what was going on; instead, you just got a feeling for what it was like when you were 10. That makes you a kinesthetic.

Assume that people are visual unless you have something else to go on. Assume that what they see has more impact than what they hear. That's why it's so important to respond to a proposal from the other side with a Flinch. Don't dismiss Flinching as childish or too theatrical until you've had a chance to see how effective it can be. It's so effective that it usually surprises our students when they first use it.

Mike once Flinched during the negotiation of a large loan from one of his banks and gained a percent rate reduction in the loan without even having to ask for it. Although he had not discussed the financing with another lender, the bank perceived his Flinch as indicating that he had been offered a better deal by another bank.

Key Points to Remember

- Flinch in reaction to a proposal from the other side. The people on the other side may not expect to get what they're asking for, but if you don't show surprise, you're communicating that it's a possibility.
- A concession often follows a Flinch. If you don't Flinch, it makes the other person a tougher negotiator.
- Assume that the other person is a visual unless you have something else to go on.
- Even if you're not face to face with the other person, you should still gasp in shock and surprise. Telephone Flinches can also be very effective.

Avoid Confrontational Negotiation

What you say in the first few moments of a negotiation often sets the climate for that negotiation. The other person quickly gets a feel for whether you are working for a win-win solution, or whether you're a tough negotiator who is out for everything you can get.

That's one problem that we have with the way attorneys negotiate—they're very confrontational negotiators. You get that white envelope in the mail with black, raised lettering in the top left-hand corner and you think, "Oh, no. What is it this time?" You open the letter, and what's the first communication from them? It's a threat. They tell you what they're going to do to you if you don't give them what they want.

Be careful what you say at the beginning of the negotiation. If the seller takes a position that you totally disagree with, don't argue. Arguing always intensifies the other person's desire to prove him or herself right. You're much better off agreeing with the other person initially and then turning the statement around using the Feel, Felt, Found formula. Respond with, "I understand exactly how you *feel* about that. Many other people have *felt* exactly the same way as you do right now." (Now you have diffused that competitive spirit. You're not arguing with the person, you're agreeing with him or her.) "But you know what we have always *found*? When we take a closer look at it, we have always found that ..."

Let's look at some examples:

- The seller is in foreclosure on his first and second mortgages and is three months behind in his payments. He says, "We're applying for a homeowner's loan to bring the payments current." You know perfectly well that nobody is going to make a third mortgage to a seller who is three months behind on his payments, but if you state that point too forcefully, it would be very confrontational. Instead, you say, "I know exactly how you *feel* about that. I've spoken to so many sellers who have *felt* that they can borrow their way out of foreclosure. The problem is that once your loan is 90 days delinquent, you will *find* that your lender won't let you bring the payments current. It will settle only for a complete payoff of the loan. It's almost impossible for you to borrow that much money in your situation."

- The property has been listed with a broker, and the seller hasn't had any offers. The seller says, "No problem; when the listing expires, I'll be able to drop the price 6 percent and sell it myself." You know that that's crazy. If the brokers haven't been able to sell it at the listed price with all the access they have to buyers, the seller most likely won't be able to sell it herself. But if you come on too strong, it's confrontational. Instead, you say, "I understand exactly how you feel about that because a lot of sellers that I have dealt with have felt exactly the same way that you do right now. But you know what I have always found? I've made some good buys from For Sale By Owners, but I much prefer to work through brokers because they do so much of the work. In fact, the only reason I would consider buying directly from the seller would be if I could really get a steal on the property."

Arguing up front creates a confrontational negotiation. Get into the habit of agreeing with the other party initially and then turning the statement around.

At our seminars, we sometimes ask a person in the front row to stand up. As we hold our two hands out, with our palms facing toward the person we've asked to stand, we ask him to place his hands against ours. Once he has done that, without saying another word, we gently start to push against him. Automatically, without any instruction, he always begins to push back. People shove back when you shove them. Similarly, when you argue with someone, it makes that person want to argue back.

The other great thing about Feel, Felt, Found is that it gives you time to think. Sometimes people say things to you that are absolutely outrageous. You haven't heard anything like this before. It shocks you. You don't know what to say. If you have Feel, Felt, Found in the back of your mind, you can say, "I understand exactly how you feel about that. Many other people have felt exactly the same way. However, I have always found ..." By the time you get there, you'll have thought of something to say.

Similarly, you sometimes catch other people at a bad moment. You may be an investor who is calling to get an appointment to see the property, and the seller says to you, "If you're an investor, I don't even want to talk to you. All you'll want to do is steal my property!" You calmly say, "I understand exactly how you feel about that. Many other people have felt exactly the same way. However ..." By the time you get there, you will have recovered your composure and will know exactly what to say.

Key Points to Remember

- Don't argue with people in the early stages of the negotiation because it creates confrontation.
- Use the Feel, Felt, Found formula to turn the hostility around.
- Having Feel, Felt, Found in the back of your mind gives you time to think when the other side throws some unexpected hostility your way.

Look Out for the Reluctant Seller

One of our readers is an extremely rich and powerful investor, a man who owns real estate all over southern California. He's very successful—what you could justifiably call a heavy hitter. He likes wheeling and dealing.

As you know if you've read our earlier book *The Weekend Millionaire's Secrets to Investing in Real Estate*, we believe in buy-and-hold real estate investing.

But this investor will sell a property if he can get a great price for it. Many smaller investors bring him purchase offers for his buildings, eager to acquire one of his better-known properties. That's when this well-seasoned investor knows how to use the Reluctant Seller Gambit.

He reads the offer quietly, and when he's finished, he slides it thoughtfully back across the table, scratches above one ear, and says something like, "I don't know. Of all my properties, I have very special feelings for this one. I was thinking of keeping it and giving it to my daughter for her college graduation present, and I really don't think that I would part with it for anything less than the full asking price. You must understand; this particular property is worth a great deal to me. But look, it was good of you to bring in an offer for me, and just to be fair to you, what is the very best price that you could give me?" Many times, he will make thousands of dollars in just a few seconds using the Reluctant Seller philosophy.

Good negotiators always try to edge up the other side's negotiating range before the real negotiating ever begins.

In 1991, Donald Trump was in trouble. He was very highly leveraged in real estate, and the New York real estate market was overbuilt and about to collapse. He needed to raise cash quickly so that he could survive the coming crunch. His best opportunity was to sell the St. Moritz Hotel. He had bought it three years before from the Helmsleys for $72 million. It was just around the corner from his recently acquired flagship Plaza Hotel, so he didn't need it anymore.

Alan Bond, a brash Australian billionaire, expressed an interest. As desperately as Trump needed to sell, he still played the Reluctant Seller. "Oh, Alan, not the St. Moritz, that's my favorite property. I'm never going to sell that. I'm going to put that in trust for my grandchildren. Anything else I have is for sale; make me an offer, but not the St. Moritz. But look, Alan, just to be fair to you—what is the very best price you would give me?" Unless you realize what a Reluctant Seller is doing to you, you'll go from the low point of your negotiating range to the midpoint, or maybe even the high point, before the negotiation even starts. Alan Bond paid Trump $180 million for the St. Moritz. It gave Trump the cash he needed to survive the following real estate recession.

Roger remembers a Long Beach, California, oceanfront condominium that he bought as an investment back in 1977. The owner was asking $59,000 for it. It was a hot real estate market at the time, and he wasn't sure how eager the owner was to sell or if she had any other offers for it. So he wrote up three offers, one at $49,000, another at $54,000, and a third at $59,000. He made an appointment to meet with the seller, who had moved out of the condominium in Long Beach and was now living in Pasadena. After talking to her for a while, Roger determined that she hadn't had any other offers and that she was eager to sell. He reached into his briefcase, where he had the three offers carefully filed, and pulled out the lowest of them. She accepted it, and when Roger sold the condominium a few years later, it fetched $129,000. (Be aware that you can do this only with a For Sale By Owner. If a real estate agent has listed the property, that agent is probably working for the seller and is obligated to tell the seller if he's aware that the other side would pay more. That's another reason we suggest listing property with an agent when you're selling.)

Note how low the prices seem in that example from 1977. Today's prices will seem just as ridiculously low 30 years from now. If Roger had kept the condo and rented it out instead of selling it, the loan would now be paid off, the property would be worth $500,000, and it would be generating $3,000 a month in rental income. Examples like this one are the reasons we now encourage people to buy and hold properties and let the income build up over time. Although he made $80,000 on the transaction, Roger's profit was capped at the time of the sale. Had he kept the condo, at today's rental rate of $3,000 per month, it would bring in this amount in just a little over two years. He would have an income stream that inflation would continue to increase, and he would have it for the rest of his life.

Look out for the Reluctant Seller when you're trying to buy a property.

Key Points to Remember

- Look out for the Reluctant Seller.
- Don't change your opening negotiating position. The seller may be trying to squeeze the negotiating range before the negotiations even start.

Play the Reluctant Buyer

Playing Reluctant Buyer is a terrific way for you to squeeze the seller's expectations before the negotiations even start. Try it and you'll see how you can get sellers to drop their price many thousands of dollars in just a few seconds.

Remember that the first price that sellers will give you is what we call the "wish price." This is what the sellers wish you would pay for the property. As a real estate investor, you can't make money buying at the wish price. You need to find out the sellers' walk-away price—the price at which they will not, or cannot, sell the property.

To do this, you need to spend time with the sellers so that they open up to you. Ask questions about how long they have had the property and what they plan to do after they've sold it. Try to find common interests like baseball, fishing, or travel. Use the property checklist from the "Downloads" section of our Web site (*www.weekendmillionaire.com*) to take extensive notes about the property.

When you cannot think of another thing to ask, and only then, you use the Reluctant Buyer Gambit and say, "I really appreciate all the time that you've taken with me. Unfortunately, I don't think I can make this work for me. Remember that I'm a real estate investor, and I need to buy properties so that I can rent them out and make a profit. At this price, I just don't think I can make it work. But I really appreciate all the time you've taken with me, and I wish you the best of luck."

You turn to leave and then, almost as an afterthought, you turn back and say, "I really appreciate all the time you have taken with me. Just to be fair to you, what is the very lowest price you would take for the property?"

Remember that this is not the end of the negotiation. It is not even the beginning of the negotiation. At this point, you're simply trying to squeeze the seller's expectations before the negotiations even start.

You won't get sellers to come all the way down from their wish price to their walk-away price by playing Reluctant Buyer, but what they will typically do is give away half their negotiating range just because you used this technique. It gives you a feel for how low they may go if you keep on negotiating.

Key Points to Remember

- Always play Reluctant Buyer.
- Look out for the Reluctant Seller.
- Playing this gambit is a great way to squeeze the other side's negotiating range before the negotiation even starts.
- The other person will typically give away half of his or her negotiating range just because you use this technique.

Use the Vise Technique

The Vise is another very effective negotiating gambit, and what it will accomplish will amaze you. The Vise Gambit is the simple little expression: "You'll have to do better than that." Here's how good negotiators use it: You have toured the property with the sellers. You have asked all the questions you can think of. You have played Reluctant Buyer to squeeze the sellers' negotiating range, and finally the sellers give you their absolute, rock bottom, can't go a penny less price for the property.

You pause, appear to study their offer, then respond with the Vise Gambit by calmly saying, "I'm sorry, you'll have to do better than that."

An experienced negotiator will automatically respond with the Counter Gambit, which is, "Exactly how much better than that do I have to do?" to try to pin you down to a specific number. However, it will amaze you how often inexperienced sellers will concede a big chunk of their negotiating range simply because you said, "You'll have to do better that that."

Mike once used this gambit on a salesperson who was trying to get him to renew an advertising contract on the cover of a city directory. When he gave Mike the renewal price, Mike very calmly said, "I'm willing to renew the contract, but you'll have to do better than that." The salesperson immediately dropped the price by about 20 percent.

Mike thought to himself, "Umh, I wonder if he'll drop the price further if I do that again." Once again he repeated the same words, "I'm willing to renew the contract, but you'll have to do better than that." The salesperson once again dropped the price, this time by about 10 percent.

Mike, sensing that the salesperson was under pressure to renew the contract and realizing that he had been given the authority to renegotiate the rate, kept using the same exact words to secure additional price reductions of 8 percent, 5 percent, and 3 percent before he finally agreed to the renewal. During this time the salesperson became increasingly nervous and even began to perspire, with big droplets running down his face. During the entire time, Mike never once said that he was unwilling to pay the renewal price, and the salesperson never once asked him how much he would have to drop the price to get the renewal. The most interesting thing about this entire transaction was that Mike simply wanted to try out the Vise technique to see how the salesperson would respond.

It was a classic example of the effectiveness of using this gambit, especially in light of the fact that Mike would have renewed at the full rate if the salesperson had not dropped the price in the beginning. When he got the second concession, it became a game to see just how far the salesperson would go. Mike still isn't sure he got the lowest price, because he finally felt so sorry for the salesperson that he went ahead and signed the contract.

What's the next thing you should do, once you've said, "You'll have to do better than that"?

You guessed it: *shut up!* Don't say another word. The other side just might make a concession to you. Salespeople call this the silent close, and they all learn it during the first week that they are in the business. You make your proposal and then shut up. The other person just might say yes, so it's foolish to say another word until you find out if he or she will or won't.

Roger once watched two salespeople do the silent close on each other. He was sitting at a circular conference table with them. The salesperson on his right wanted to buy a piece of real estate from the salesperson on his left. He made his proposal and then shut up, just as they had taught him in sales training school. The more experienced salesperson on his left must have thought, "Son of a gun. I can't believe this. He's going to try the silent close on *moi*? I'll teach him a thing or two. I won't talk either."

Now Roger was sitting between two strong-willed people who were both silently daring the other to be the next one to talk. There was dead silence in the room, except for the grandfather clock ticking away in the background. Roger looked at each of them. Obviously, they both knew what was going on. Neither one was willing to give in to the other. Roger didn't know how this was ever going to be resolved. It seemed as though half an hour went by, although it was probably more like five minutes, because a period of silence seems like such a long time in our culture (see Chapter 12, "Negotiating with People from Foreign Cultures," to learn how people from other cultures will use this against us). Finally, the more experienced salesperson broke the impasse by scrawling the word "DECIZION?" on a pad of paper and sliding it across to the other. He had deliberately misspelled the word *decision*. The younger salesperson looked at it and without thinking said, "You misspelled decision." And once he started talking, he couldn't stop. (Do you know any salespeople like that? Once they start talking, they can't stop?) He went on to say, "If you're not willing to accept what I offered you, I might be willing to come up another $2,000, but not a penny more." He renegotiated his own proposal before he found out whether the other person would accept it or not.

Great negotiators use the Vise technique by simply responding to the other side's proposal or counterproposal with, "I'm sorry, you'll have to do better than that." And then shut up.

Don't fall into the trap of negotiating percentages when you should be negotiating dollars. We deal with big numbers in real estate. We might be trying to put together a $500,000 acquisition, so $2,000 might not seem significant. If we were buying a $10,000 used vehicle, $2,000 would seem like a lot of money.

If you make a $2,000 concession to a seller, it doesn't matter whether you made it on a $500,000 purchase or a $10,000 purchase. It's still $2,000 that you gave away. What you should have been thinking was, "There's $2,000 sitting in the middle of the negotiating table. How long should I be willing to spend negotiating further to see how much of it I could get?"

Have a feel for what your time's worth. Don't spend half an hour negotiating a $10 item (unless you're doing it just for the practice). Even if you got the other side to concede all of the $10, you'd be making money at the rate of only $20 an hour for the half-hour you invested in the negotiation. To put this in perspective for you, if you make $200,000 a year, you're making about $100 an hour. You should be thinking to yourself, "Is what I'm doing right now generating more than $100 per hour?" If so, it's part of the solution. If you're aimlessly chatting with someone at the water cooler, or talking about last night's television movie, or doing anything else that is not generating $100 an hour, it's part of your financial problem.

Here's the point. When you're negotiating a real estate purchase with someone—when you have a deal in front of you that you could live with, but you're wondering if you could hang in a little bit longer and do a little bit better—you're not making $100 an hour. You're making $100 a minute and maybe even $100 a second.

You will never make money faster than you will when you're negotiating well.

Key Points to Remember

- Respond to a proposal or counterproposal with the Vise technique: "You'll have to do better than that."
- If it's used on you, respond with the Counter Gambit, "Exactly how much better than that do I have to do?" This will pin the seller down to a specific number.
- Concentrate on the dollar amount that's being negotiated. Don't be distracted by the gross amount of the sale and start thinking percentages.
- Be aware of what your time is worth on an hourly basis.
- You will never make money faster than you will when you're negotiating well.

10

Middle Negotiating Gambits

As the negotiations progress, other factors come into play. In this chapter, we'll teach you the middle negotiating gambits that will keep the momentum going toward a successful conclusion.

Higher Authority

One of the most frustrating situations an investor can run into is trying to negotiate with someone who claims that he or she doesn't have the authority to make a final decision. Unless you realize that this is simply a negotiating tactic that's being used on you, you will have the feeling that you'll never get to talk to the real decision maker.

Roger used this gambit very effectively when he was president of a big real estate company in California. Salespeople would be coming in to sell him things all the time: advertising, office machines, furniture, and so on. He would always negotiate the very lowest price that he could, using all of these gambits. Then he would say to them, "This looks fine. I do just have to run it by my board of directors, but I'll get back to you tomorrow with the final okay."

The next day he could get back to them and say, "Wow, are they tough to deal with right now. I felt sure I could sell it to them, but they just won't go along with it unless you can shave another couple of hundred dollars off the price." And he would get it. In fact, there was no approval needed by the board of directors, and it never occurred to Roger that this deception was underhanded. The people with whom you are dealing see it as well within the rules by which one plays the game of negotiating.

When a seller tells you that he has to take your offer to his partners, it's probably not true, but it is a very effective negotiating tactic that he's using on you.

Let's first look at why this is such an effective tactic, and then we'll tell you how to handle it when the other side uses it on you.

Why the Seller Loves to Use Higher Authority

You would think that if you were going to negotiate something, you would want to have the authority to make a decision. At first glance, it would seem that you would have more power if you were able to say to the seller, "I have the power to make a deal with you." Good negotiators know that you put yourself in a weaker negotiating position when you say that. You should always have a higher authority with whom you have to check before you can change your proposal or make a decision. Any negotiator who presents him- or herself as the decision maker has put him- or herself at a bargaining disadvantage. You have to put your ego on the back burner to do this, but you'll find it very effective.

The reason that this tactic is so effective is simple. When the people on the other side know that you have the final authority to make a deal, they also know that you are the only person that they have to convince. They don't have to work quite as hard to give you the benefits of the proposal if you're the final authority. Once you've given your approval, they know that they have consummated the deal.

That's not so if you tell them that you have to answer to a higher authority. When you tell the sellers that you have to get approval from your partners, the sellers have to do more to convince you. They must make an offer that you can take to your partners and get approved. They know that they must completely win you over so that you will want to persuade your partners to agree to the proposal.

Higher Authority works much better when the higher authority is a vague entity such as partners or a board of directors. For example, have you ever actually met a loan committee at a bank? We never have. Bankers have consistently told us that for loans of $500,000 or less, somebody at that bank can make a decision without having to go to the loan committee. However, the loan officer knows that if she said to you, "Your package is on the vice president's desk," you would say, "Well, let's go talk to the vice president right now. Let's get it resolved." You can't do that with a vague entity.

If you use the Higher Authority Gambit, then, be sure that your higher authority is a vague entity, such as partners or a board of directors. If you tell the other person that your partner would have to approve it, what's the first thought that he or she is going to have? Right. "Then why am I wasting time talking to you? If your partner is the only one who can make a decision, get your partner down here." However, when your higher authority is a vague entity, it appears to be unapproachable. In all the years that Roger told salespeople that he had to run proposals by his board of directors, he only once had a salesperson say to him, "When does your board of directors meet? When can I make a presentation to them?" The use of Higher Authority is a great way of putting pressure on people without confrontation.

When Roger first bought rental properties, it felt great to him to tell the tenants that he owned the property. It was an ego trip for him. But when his portfolio became substantial, he realized that it wasn't that much fun anymore, because the tenants assumed that the owner of the property was made of money. Why would it be a problem for him to replace the carpeting in their unit because of a small cigarette burn, or to replace the drapes because of a small tear? Why would it be a problem if the rent was late that month? In their eyes, Roger was rich. He must be, because he had all that property. Why was this upsetting him?

The moment he learned the power of the Higher Authority Gambit and started a company that he called Plaza Properties, many of these problems went away. He became the president of a company that was, to the tenants, a property management company handling their building for a vague group of investors out there somewhere.

Then when they said, "We've got this cigarette burn in the carpet, and it needs to be replaced," he'd say, "I don't think I can get the owners to do that for you just yet. I'll tell you what, though, you keep the rent coming in on the first of the month, and in about six months, I'll go to bat for you with the owners. Let me see what I can do for you with them at that time."

If they said, "Roger, we're not going to have the rent until the fifteenth of the month," he would say, "Wow, I know exactly how it goes. Sometimes it can get difficult, but unfortunately, on this property I just don't have any leeway. The owners of this property told me that if the rent's not in by the fifth of the month, I have to file an eviction. What can we do to get the rent in on time?"

Here's another reason why we recommend that you always use property managers. Not only does it free up your time to look for more properties and save you the frustration of dealing with tenants, but property managers can put more pressure on tenants without being confrontational.

We're sure you can see why the other person loves using this gambit on you. Look at the benefits to sellers when they tell you that they have to get your proposal approved by their partners:

- They can put pressure on you without confrontation: "I'd be wasting our time taking an offer that low to my partners."
- This gambit unbalances you as a negotiator because it's so frustrating to feel that you're not able to present your offer to the real decision maker.
- By inventing a higher authority, they can set aside the pressure of making a decision. As a real estate broker, Roger would teach his agents that before they put buyers in their cars to show them property, they should say to them, "Just to be sure I understand, if we find exactly the right home for you today, is there any reason why you wouldn't make a decision today?" What this accomplished was that it eliminated the buyers' right, under the pressure of the closing situation, to delay by inventing a higher authority. If the agent didn't do this, buyers would very often defer the decision by saying, "We can't decide today because Uncle Harry is helping us with the down payment, and we have to run it by him."
- It sets them up for using the Vise technique: "You'll have to do better than that if you want to get it past my partners."
- It puts you in the position of needing to have them on your side to get the deal approved by their partners.
- They can make suggestions to you without implying that this is something to which they'd agree: "If you can come down another 10 percent, you may have a chance of my partners approving it."
- It can be used to force you into a bidding war: "My partners have asked me to get three offers, and it looks as though they're going to take the highest one."
- They can squeeze your price without revealing what you're up against: "The partners are meeting tomorrow to make a final decision. I know they've already gotten some really good offers, so there may not be any point in you submitting

yours, but there's always a chance if you can come in with a high offer."

- It sets the other person up to use Good Guy/Bad Guy: "If it were up to me, I'd love to keep on doing business with you, but my partners only care about the highest price."

The Counter Gambits to Higher Authority

You can see why sellers and bankers love to use the Higher Authority Gambit on you. Fortunately, good negotiators know how to handle this challenge smoothly and effectively.

Your first approach should be to try to remove the other person's resort to higher authority before the negotiations even start, by getting the other person to admit that he or she could make a decision if the proposal was irresistible. This is exactly the same thing that Roger taught his real estate agents to say to the buyers before putting them in the car, "Let me be sure I understand. If we find exactly the right property for you today, is there any reason why you wouldn't make a decision today?"

One of the most frustrating things that you encounter is taking your proposal to the other person and having her say to you, "Well, that's fine. Thanks for bringing me the proposal. I'll talk to my partners (or my attorney) about it, and if it interests us, we'll get back to you." Where do you go from there? If you're smart enough to counter the Higher Authority Gambit before you start, you can remove yourself from that danger.

Before you present your proposal to the other person, before you even get it out of your briefcase, you should casually say to him or her, "Let me be sure I understand. If this proposal meets all of your needs," (that's as broad as any statement can be, isn't it?) "is there any reason why you wouldn't give me a decision today?"

To the other person, this seems like a harmless thing to agree to because he or she is thinking, "If it meets all of my needs? No problem, there's loads of wriggle room there. I can always find something to object to." However, look at what you've accomplished if you can get someone to respond with, "Well, sure, if it meets *all* of my needs, I'll give you an okay right now." Look at what you've accomplished:

1. You've eliminated the person's right to tell you that he or she wants to think it over. If the person says that, you say, "Well, let me go over it one more time. There must be something I didn't cover clearly enough because you did indicate to me earlier that you were willing to make a decision today."

2. You've eliminated the person's right to refer your proposal to a higher authority. You've eliminated his or her right to say, "I want my lawyer to see it, or my partners to take a look at it."

What if you're not able to remove the resort to higher authority? I'm sure that many times you'll say, "If this proposal meets all of your needs, is there any reason why you can't give me a decision today?" and the seller will reply, "I'm sorry, but my partners are involved in this. I'll have to refer it to them for a final decision."

Here are the three steps that good negotiators take when they're not able to remove the other side's resort to higher authority:

Step 1: Appeal to their ego. With a smile on your face, you say, "But your partners always follow your recommendations, don't they?" With some personality styles, that is enough of an appeal to the ego to get the seller to say, "Well, I guess you're right. If I approve it, then you can count on it." But often the other person will still say, "Yes, they usually follow my recommendations, but I can't give you a decision until I've taken it to them."

Step 2: Get their commitment to recommending it. You say, "But you will recommend it to them, won't you?" Hopefully, you'll get a response similar to, "Yes, it looks good to me. I'll go to bat for you with them."

Getting the other side's commitment to recommending your proposal to the higher authority is very important because it's at this point that the person may reveal that there really isn't a committee. He or she really does have the authority to make a decision, and saying that he or she had to check with someone else was just a negotiating gambit that was being used on you.

In step 2, then, smart negotiators get the seller's commitment to going to the higher authority with a positive recommendation. There are only two things that can happen now. Either the seller will say, "Yes, I will recommend it to them," or the seller will say, "No, I won't recommend it because ...," and either way you've won. The endorsement would be preferable, of course, but any time you can draw out an objection, you should say "Hallelujah" because objections are buying signals. Sellers are not going to object to your offer price unless selling to you interests them. If selling to you doesn't interest them, they don't care how close to their asking price your offer is.

Objections are buying signals. Roger knew that in real estate sales, if his agents were showing property, and the people were oohing and aahing all over the place, if they loved everything about the property, they weren't going to buy. The serious buyers were the ones who were saying, "Well, the kitchen's not as big as we'd like. Hate that wallpaper. We'd probably end up knocking out that wall." Those were the ones who would buy.

If you're in sales, think about it. Have you ever in your life made a big sale where the person loved your price up front? Of course not. All serious buyers complain about the price.

Objections are buying signals. When you say to a seller, "You will recommend it to your partners, won't you?" the seller can say either yes or no. Either way you've won. Then you can move to step 3.

> *Step 3: The qualified "subject to" close.* The qualified "subject to" close in this instance would be: "Let's just write up the paperwork subject to the right of your CPA to reject the proposal within a 24-hour period for any tax reason." Or, "Let's just write up the paperwork subject to the right of your legal department to reject the proposal within a 24-hour period for any legal reason."

Notice that you're not saying subject to anyone's acceptance. You're saying subject to the right to decline it for a specific reason. If the other person is going to refer it to an attorney, it would be a legal reason. If he or she is going to refer it to a CPA, it would be a tax reason, and so on. But try to get it nailed down to a specific reason.

So the three steps to take if you're not able to get the other person to waive his or her resort to higher authority are:

1. Appeal to the other person's ego.
2. Get the other person's commitment to recommending your proposal to the higher authority.
3. Use the qualified subject-to close.

What's the counter to the counter gambit? What if someone is trying to remove your resort to higher authority that way? If the other person says to you, "You do have the authority to make a decision, don't you?" you should say, in so many words, "It depends on what you're asking. There's a point at which I have to go to my partners."

Being able to use and handle the resort to higher authority is critical to you when you're negotiating. Always maintain your own resort to higher authority. Always try to remove the other person's resort to a higher authority.

Key Points to Remember

- Don't let the other side know that you have the authority to make a decision.
- Your higher authority should be a vague entity, not an individual.
- Leave your ego at home when you're negotiating. Don't let the seller trick you into admitting that you have authority.
- Attempt to get the other party to admit that he or she could approve your proposal if it meets all of his or her needs. If that fails, go through the three counter gambits:
  1. Appeal to the seller's ego.
  2. Get a commitment to recommend your proposal to the higher authority.
  3. Go to a qualified subject-to close.

Never Offer to Split the Difference

In this country, we have a tremendous sense of fair play. This sense of fair play tells us that if both sides give equally in a negotiation, then the result is fair. If Fred puts his house up for sale at $200,000, Susan makes an offer at $190,000, and both Fred and Susan are eager to compromise, both of them tend to be thinking, "If we settled at $195,000, that would be fair, because we both gave equally."

Maybe it's fair and maybe it isn't. It depends on the opening negotiating positions that Fred and Susan took. If the house is really worth $190,000 and Fred is holding to his overinflated price only to take advantage of Susan's having fallen in love with the property, then it's not fair. If the house is worth $200,000 and Susan is willing to pay that, but is taking advantage of Fred's financial problems, then it isn't fair. So, don't fall into the trap of thinking that splitting the difference is the fair thing to do when you can't resolve a difference in price with the other side. (A word about terminology here. Real estate agents sell "houses," but buyers buy "homes." When you're dealing with a seller, tone down his or her emotional attachment to the property by referring to it as a house. When your property manager is dealing with a potential renter, he or she should turn up the emotional attachment by renting that person a home.)

Remember that splitting the difference doesn't always mean down the middle.

If you are at $220,000 and the seller is at $240,000 and you split the difference once, you'd be at $230,000. Get the seller to split the difference again, and you'd be at $225,000; once more, and you'd be at $222,500.

Here's how to use this gambit.

The first thing to remember is that you should never offer to split the difference yourself, but you should always encourage the other person to offer to split the difference.

Let's say that you're trying to buy a fourplex (a four-unit apartment building). The seller is asking $600,000, and you've offered $540,000. The negotiations have gone back and forth for several weeks, and now you are at $560,000 and the seller has come down to $570,000, so you're only $10,000 apart.

Where do you go from there? You have a strong feeling that if you offered to split the difference, the seller would agree to do so, which would mean agreeing at $565,000.

Instead of offering to split the difference, encourage the seller to offer to split the difference. You say, "Well, I guess this is just not going to fly. It seems like such a shame, though, when we've both spent so much time working on this." (Remember what we told you earlier about how people become more flexible the longer they've been negotiating.) "We've spent so much time on this, and we've come so close to a price that we could both live with. It seems like a shame that it's all going to collapse when we're only $10,000 apart."

If you keep stressing the amount of time that you've spent on it and the small amount of money that you're apart on the price, eventually the seller will say, "Look, why don't we just split the difference?"

You act dumb and say, "Let's see, splitting the difference, what would that mean? I'm at $560,000 and you're at $570,000. What you're telling me is that you'd go down to $565,000? Is that what I hear you saying?"

"Well, yes," the seller says. "If you'll come up to $565,000, then we'll settle for that."

So you say, "$565,000 sounds a lot better than $570,000. Tell you what, let me talk to my partners" (or whatever other higher authority you've set up) "and see how they feel about it. I'll tell them you came down to $565,000, and we'll see if we can't put the deal together. I'll get back to you tomorrow."

The next day you get back to the seller and you say, "Wow, are my partners tough to deal with right now. I felt sure that I could get them to go along with $565,000, but we spent two hours last night going over the figures again, and they insist that we'll lose money if we go a penny above $560,000. But golly! We're only $5,000 apart on this now. Surely, we're not going to let it all fall apart when we're only $5,000 apart?"

If you keep that up long enough, eventually the seller will offer to split the difference again.

If you are able to get the seller to split the difference again, this gambit has made you an extra $2,500 of bottom-line profit. However, even if you can't get the seller to split the difference again and you end up at the same $565,000 that you would have paid if *you* had offered to split the difference, something very significant has happened here. Can you see what the significant thing that happened was?

Right! The seller now feels that he won because you got *him* to propose splitting the difference at $565,000. Then you got your partners to reluctantly agree to a proposal that the other side had made. If *you* had suggested splitting the difference, then it would have put the seller in the position of having to come down to $565,000, which to him would be coming down to meet a proposal that you had made.

That may seem like a very subtle thing, but it's very significant in terms of who felt they won and who felt they lost. Remember that the essence of good negotiating is to always leave the other side feeling that they won.

The rule is, never offer to Split the Difference, but always encourage the other person to offer to Split the Difference.

Key Points to Remember

- Don't fall into the trap of thinking that splitting the difference is the fair thing to do.
- Splitting the difference doesn't mean down the middle because you can do it more than once.
- Never offer to split the difference yourself; instead, encourage the other person to offer to split the difference.
- By getting the seller to offer to split the difference, you put the seller in the position of suggesting the compromise. Then you can reluctantly agree to that proposal, making the seller feel that he or she won.

Don't Let Other People Give You Their Problems

As a real estate investor, you will find a lot of people who will try to give you what are essentially their problems.

You will hear:

"That won't leave me enough to pay the real estate broker."

"That's not enough to pay off the existing loan."

"That's not enough for the down payment on our new condo in Florida."

What you should do is the same thing that international negotiators would tell you to do when the other side tries to give you its problems. We've found out from our study of international negotiations that exactly the same principles apply—the same rules that applied for the negotiators in Geneva during the arms control talks also apply to you in your real estate negotiations when the other side is putting pressure on you. Not only do the same principles apply, but the same responses are appropriate.

Here's how the international negotiators would tell you to respond to the Hot Potato: test it for validity right away. This is what international negotiators do when the other side tries to give them its problem. You have to find out right away whether this really is a deal killer that's been tossed to you, or whether it's simply something that's been thrown onto the negotiating table to judge your response.

You must jump on it right away. Later is too late. If you work on the problem, the other side will soon believe that it's now your problem, and it's too late to test it for validity.

Real estate agents get tossed the Hot Potato all the time, such as the buyer who says: "We have only $10,000 to put down." Even in blue-collar areas, that would be a very low down payment. The real estate agent could possibly work with it, but it would be tough.

Roger would teach his agents to test this statement for validity right away—to say to the buyers, "Maybe we can work with $10,000. But let me ask you this: if I find exactly the right property for you, in exactly the right neighborhood, the price and terms are fantastic, your family is going to love it, your kids are going to love having their friends over to play, but it takes $15,000 to get in—is there any point in my showing it to you, or should I just show it to my other buyers?"

Once in a great while they would respond, "Don't you speak English? Read my lips: $10,000 is it and not a penny more. I don't care how good a buy it is."

But nine times out of ten they would say, "Well, we didn't want to touch our certificate of deposit, but if it's a really good buy we might. Or maybe Uncle Joe would help us with the down payment." Immediately the agent found out that the problem the buyers had tossed her was not the deal killer that it had appeared to be.

Nine times out of ten they'd say, "Sure, we'll take a look at it," and immediately you'd know that the price issue was not the deal buster that it appeared to be.

Perhaps the bank loan officer has told you, "Our bank rules don't allow us to loan you that much." You test this for validity by saying, "Who at your bank can waive that rule?"

Sometime you'll kick yourself at what happens next. The loan officer says, "Well, it would take a vice president to authorize that." And you say, "Well, you want to do it, don't you? Why don't you call the vice president and see if you can get an okay to waive the rule?" The loan officer may just pick up the telephone, call the vice president, and argue for an okay. Sometimes it's that simple. But you have to test for validity right away.

Roger remembers doing a seminar for the Associated General Contractors of Alaska. They put him up at the Anchorage Hilton, and on his departure day, he needed a late checkout. There were two young people standing right next to each other behind the registration desk, and he said to one of them: "Would you give me a 6 o'clock checkout in my room, please."

She said, "Mr. Dawson, we could do that for you, but we'd have to charge you for an extra half day."

Roger (testing for validity) said, "Who would have the authority to waive that charge?"

The clerk pointed to the person standing next to her and said, "She would." The person standing right next to her!

So Roger leaned over and said to the other clerk, "And how would you feel about that?"

She hesitated for a moment and then said, "Oh, sure. That would be fine. Go ahead."

Let's take a look at the three seller problems we mentioned earlier and see how we can test for validity:

"That won't leave me enough to pay the real estate broker."
Response: *"Have you asked the broker to reduce the commission?"*

"That's not enough to pay off the existing loan."
Response: *"Have you approached the lender about a short sale?"* (A word about short sales: if the lender has a delinquent loan on its hands, it will often accept less to pay off the loan. There is no magic to this. The seller sends or takes your offer to the lender and asks it to accept the proceeds of the sale as payment in full.)

"That's not enough for the down payment on our new condo in Florida."
Response: *"Have you asked the builders if they would accept a lower down payment?"*

The key point here is to understand the difficulties the sellers may be having, but not to take responsibility for their problems. Many times the sellers' problem is the result of a lack of knowledge about the options that are available to them. The more you know about the sellers, the more you will be able to structure your offers to their needs, but don't let the sellers' problems become yours. Learn to toss the problems back to them by testing for validity.

Another way to handle the "we don't have it in the budget" Hot Potato is to ask them when their budget year ends. This gambit once made Roger $5,200. He had been hired to train the 80 salespeople at one of the top HMOs in California. A few weeks before the meeting, the training director called him and suggested that they have dinner so that she could fill Roger in on how the company operates. They went to the top French restaurant in Orange County and had a great dinner. As dessert was being served, Roger said to the training director, "You know what you should do? You should invest in a set of my audio programs for each of your salespeople so that they have the advantage of a continuous learning process." As he said that, he was mentally calculating that 80 salespeople at $65 per program would be another $5,200 in income on top of the speaking fee to which they'd already agreed.

She thought about it and said, "Roger, that probably would be a good idea, but we just don't have it in the budget."

Roger tested for validity. He asked, "When does your budget year end?" This was August, and he thought that she would tell him December 31.

To his surprise, she said, "At the end of September."

"So you would have it in the budget on October 1?"

"Yes, I suppose we would."

"Then, no problem; I'll ship you the audio programs and bill you on October 1, fair enough?"

"That would be fine," she told him. In less than 30 seconds, he had made a $5,200 sale because he knew that when she tossed him what was essentially her problem, he should test for validity.

Look out for people giving you their problems. You have enough problems of your own, don't you? It's like the businessman who was pacing the floor at night. He couldn't sleep, and his wife was getting frantic. "Darling, what's bothering you? Why don't you come to bed?" He said, "Well, we have this huge loan payment due tomorrow, and the bank manager is a good friend of ours. I just hate to have to face him and say that we're not going to have the money to pay him."

His wife picked up the telephone, called their friend the bank manager, and said, "That loan payment we have coming due tomorrow, we don't have the money to pay it."

The husband exploded. He said, "What did you do that for? That's what I was afraid of."

And she said: "Well, dear, now it's his problem, and you can come to bed."

Don't let other people give you their problems.

> ## Key Points to Remember
>
> - When the seller tries to give you what is essentially his or her problem, test it for validity right away.
> - If the real estate agent or banker tries to get you to believe that what you are proposing is against their organization's rules, ask who has the authority to change the rules.
> - If they say your proposal is not permitted under their procedures, ask who at their organization can change procedure.
> - Don't let other people toss you their problems. Test for validity right away.

The Declining Value of Services

Here's something that you can expect when dealing with another person: any concession you make to that person will quickly lose its value. The value of any material object you buy may go up in value over the years because of inflation or scarcity, but the value of services always appears to decline rapidly after you have performed those services.

This teaches you that any time you make a concession to the other side in a negotiation, you should ask for a reciprocal concession right away. The favor that you extended to the other side loses value very quickly.

Real estate salespeople are very familiar with the principle of the declining value of services. When a seller has a problem getting rid of a property, and the real estate salesperson offers to solve that problem for a 6 percent listing fee, it doesn't sound as though that's an enormous amount of money. However, the minute the real estate agent has performed the service by finding a buyer, that 6 percent suddenly starts to sound like a tremendous amount of money. "Wait a minute, 6 percent—that's $12,000," the seller is saying. "For what? What did she do? All she did was put it in a Multiple Listing Service." In fact, the real estate agent did much more than that to market the property and negotiate the contract, but remember the principle: the value of a service always appears to diminish rapidly after you have performed that service.

You've reached agreement on the purchase of a rental house, and you're on good terms with the sellers. They call you just before closing and ask if they could stay in the property one more week because the condo they're moving to isn't ready yet. You had scheduled two weeks to refurbish the property, but you really need only one week. You let them stay as long as they promise to leave the property in perfect condition. They really appreciate what you did for them, and they promise that the property's condition will be perfect. But when they move out, the place is a disaster. The value of the service you performed for them went down quickly. (A word of advice here: evicting people from property is difficult in these days of liberal-minded courts. This is an area where you need to be a tough-minded businessperson. On the day the property closes, you need to verify that the former occupants are out and that you're going to get possession of the property. It's always a good idea to drive by the property for a quick inspection on the way to the closing, if possible. If you can't verify the property's condition, delay the closing until you can.)

The rule of the declining value of services tells you that if you make a concession during a negotiation, you need to get a reciprocal concession right away. Don't wait. Don't be sitting there thinking that because you did them a favor, they owe you and they will make it up to you later. With all the goodwill in the world, the value of what you did goes down rapidly in their mind if you wait.

For the same reason, service providers know that you should always negotiate your fee up front, not afterward.

Plumbers know this, don't they? They know that the time to negotiate with you is before they do the work, not after. Roger had a plumber out to his house. After looking at the problem he slowly shook his head and said, "Mr. Dawson, I have identified the problem, and I can fix it for you. It will cost you $150."

He said, "Fine, go ahead."

You know how long it took him to do the work? Five minutes. Roger said, "Now wait a minute. You're going to charge me $150 for five minutes' work? I'm a nationally known speaker, and I don't make that kind of money."

He replied, "Well, I didn't make that kind of money either when I was a nationally known speaker."

Key Points to Remember

- The value of a material object may go up over time, but the value of services always appears to go down.
- Don't make a concession and trust that the other side will make it up to you later.
- If you're providing a service, negotiate your fee before you do the work.

How to Handle Impasses

In extended negotiations, you will frequently encounter impasses, stalemates, and deadlocks in your negotiations with people. Here's how we define the three terms:

- *Impasse*. You are in complete disagreement on one issue, and it threatens the negotiations.
- *Stalemate*. Both sides are still talking, but they seem to be unable to make any progress toward a solution.
- *Deadlock*. The lack of progress has frustrated both sides so much that they see no point in talking to each other any more.

It's easy for an inexperienced negotiator to confuse an impasse with a deadlock:

- The sellers want all cash for the property. You need them to carry back some financing to make the numbers work.

- The sellers need to close the deal by the end of the month, and you need more time to pull the financing together.
- You're 20 percent apart on the price of the house.

All of these may sound like deadlocks to the inexperienced negotiator, but to a good negotiator, they're only impasses. You can use a very easy gambit whenever you reach an impasse. It's called the Set-Aside Gambit.

What you should do is set aside the major issue and search for agreement on little issues. After you've created momentum in the negotiations, you return to the major issue. You'll find that it is now much easier to resolve.

You might say to the seller, "Okay, I understand that we're $20,000 apart on the price, but let's set that issue aside for a moment and take a look at some of the other issues involved. When would you want to close on the property?" (A word about closing dates here. As a buyer, you want to delay the closing date as long as you can. If the sellers don't want to close until next year when their child graduates from college, that's fine with you, because you're getting the ultimate leverage. You may have to put up only a $1,000 earnest money deposit, and you're controlling a $300,000 property for nine months. What's wrong with that? Realize that the seller probably assumes that you want to close as quickly as you can. This is another area where both sides can win because they don't see things from the same point of view.)

The sellers might respond very adversely to your suggestion that they carry back financing. They tell you, "Absolutely not. We will never take back a note on our property. We want cash! If you want us to carry back financing, forget about it!" Don't panic or react emotionally. Calmly say, "Okay, I understand. Let's just set that issue aside for a while and take a look at some of these other issues."

Mike used this gambit to make his first purchase, in which the seller financed a substantial portion of the sales price for 10 years at 0 percent interest. His original offer was for full price, even though he would have had to pay substantially less if he had been required to use conventional bank financing. The seller's initial reaction was, "Absolutely not! I'm leaving the area, and I need all cash."

Mike then said, "Well, let's set aside the idea of seller financing and see how much I can pay if I have to give you cash." When he returned with another offer that was several thousand dollars less than his original offer, the seller was very offended and wanted to know why he couldn't pay the asking price. This led to a lengthy discussion in which they agreed that Mike would purchase the stove and refrigerator for $100 each, and the seller would throw in the curtains in the living room and agree to leave the new vacuum cleaner that Mike had seen in the house during his inspection.

Eventually the discussion came back to the price. Mike asked the seller what she intended to do with the money if he paid her cash. She responded that she would put it in a bank deposit account and use the interest from it to supplement her income. Mike then pointed out that what she could earn in interest would be far less than what he would pay her each month if she accepted his higher price and financed the purchase at 0 percent interest. (This type of arrangement works only if you plan to keep the property until it is paid off or you insert an assumption clause in the loan. By paying a higher price and offering 0 percent interest, you are in effect building some amount of interest into the price.)

Although the seller had been totally opposed to taking back a note in the beginning, after working out several smaller details, she felt better about financing the purchase, and Mike was able to buy the house for the amount he had offered in the beginning.

When you use the Set-Aside Gambit, you resolve many of the little issues first to establish some momentum in the negotiation before leading up to the big issues. As we'll teach you in Chapter 14, "The Art of Win-Win Negotiating," don't narrow things down to just one issue (when there's only one issue on the table, there has to be a winner and there has to be a loser). By resolving the little issues first, you create momentum that will make the big issues much easier to resolve. Inexperienced negotiators always seem to think that you need to resolve the big issues first. "If we can't get together on the major things like price and terms, why waste much time talking to them about the little issues?" Good negotiators understand that the other side will become much more flexible after you've reached agreement on the small issues.

Key Points to Remember

- Don't confuse an impasse with a deadlock. True deadlocks are very rare, so what you've reached is probably only an impasse.
- Handle an impasse with the Set-Aside Gambit: "Let's just set that aside for a moment and talk about some of the other issues, may we?"
- Create momentum by resolving minor issues first, but don't narrow the negotiation down to only one issue. For more on this, see Chapter 14.

Handling Stalemates

Somewhere between an impasse and a deadlock, you will sometimes encounter a stalemate. That's when both sides are still talking, but they are unable to make any progress toward a solution.

Being in a stalemate is similar to being "in irons," which is a sailing expression meaning that the boat has stalled with its head into the wind. A sailboat will not sail directly into the wind. It will sail almost into the wind, but it won't sail directly into it. To sail into the wind, you must sail about 30 degrees off course to starboard and then tack across the wind 30 degrees to port. It's hard work to keep resetting the sails that way, but eventually you'll get where you want to go. To tack across the wind, you must keep the bow of the boat moving smoothly through the wind. If you hesitate, you can get stuck with your bow into the wind. If you lose momentum as you tack, there may not be enough wind to move the bow of the boat around. When a skipper is in irons, he or she has to do something to correct the problem—perhaps reset the sails, back up the jib sail to pull the bow around, waggle the tiller or wheel, or do something else that will regain momentum. Similarly, when negotiations stall, you must change the dynamics to reestablish momentum. Here are some things that you can do, other than changing the monetary amount involved:

- Change the people on the negotiating team. A favorite expression that attorneys use is, "I have to be in court this afternoon, so my partner Charlie will be taking my place." The court may be a tennis court, but it's a tactful way of changing the team.

- Remove a member who may have irritated the other side. A sophisticated negotiator won't take offense at being asked to leave because he or she has played a valuable role as a Bad Guy. Now it's time to alternate the pressure on the other side by making the concession of removing this person from your team. If you haven't been able to make progress with the sellers, try having your partner or your spouse approach them.

- Change the venue by suggesting that you continue the discussion over lunch or dinner.

- Ease the tension by talking about the sellers' hobbies or a piece of gossip in the news or by telling a funny story.

- Explore the possibility of a change in finances, such as raising (or lowering) the down payment, an increased earnest money deposit, or restructured financing. Any of these may be enough to change the dynamics and move you out of the stalemate. Remember that the other side may be reluctant to raise these issues for fear of appearing to be in poor financial condition.

- Try changing the ambiance in the negotiating room. If the negotiations have been low key with an emphasis on win-win, try becoming more competitive. If the negotiations have been hard driving, try switching to more of a win-win mode.

Middle Negotiating Gambits

When a sailboat is in irons, the skipper may not know exactly how to regain momentum, so sometimes he or she simply has to try different things to see what works. If negotiations reach a stalemate, you have to try different things to see what will regain momentum for you. Something will happen when you change the dynamics in an attempt to create momentum, but you're never sure what it will be.

Mike found himself in a stalemate when he was trying to negotiate a settlement with an insurance company. His airplane had been damaged by a hailstorm while it was parked on the ground. Mike wanted the damaged skins replaced at a cost of more than $210,000, but the insurance company wanted to only repair them (sort of like filling dings in a car and then repainting it) at a cost of $98,000. Both sides had been negotiating through their attorneys. The insurance company had come up to $135,000, and Mike's attorney had offered to settle for $155,000. Several days passed, and neither side would budge.

At this point, Mike told his attorney that he wanted to settle the matter, but that the attorneys didn't seem to be making any progress. He asked his attorney to contact the insurance company's attorney and see if there was someone with the authority to settle the matter who would talk with him directly. Within a few days, he received a call from the chief adjustor of the insurance company. Mike said that he could make a final decision on his side and asked the adjustor if he was authorized to do the same for the insurance company. The adjustor assured Mike that he could also make a decision.

Mike then explained to the adjustor that the damage to his plane was more than $210,000 and that all he had been offered by the insurance company was $135,000. (Note: In his opening statement, Mike used the highest amount the insurance company's attorney had offered as the company's starting point, but he went back to the original estimate for new skins, or $210,000, as his starting position.) To his surprise, the adjustor never questioned either position, but instead asked how they could reach an agreement. He then went on to say that he wanted to be fair and that he was willing to raise the offer to $160,000 if the matter could be settled that day.

Mike said that he appreciated the offer and also wanted to resolve the matter. He offered to lower the amount he would accept to $185,000 if a deal could be reached. (He lowered what he would accept by the same amount that the adjustor had raised the amount the insurance company was offering to pay.) This now left them $25,000 apart, but the company's offer was $25,000 more than had been offered through its attorney. Believe it or not, it took them less than an hour of making increasingly smaller and smaller concessions to arrive at a final figure of $175,000 to settle the claim.

Both parties left the negotiation feeling that they had won. Mike got $40,000 more than the best offer the insurance company's attorney had made to his attorney, and the adjustor settled the claim for $35,000 less than what Mike had originally wanted. Although many different tactics came into play in this negotiation, the stalemate was broken when each side changed negotiators.

Key Points to Remember

- Be aware of the difference between an impasse, a stalemate, and a deadlock. In a stalemate, both sides still want to find a solution, but neither can see a way to move forward.
- The response to a stalemate should be to change the dynamics of the negotiation by altering one of the elements.

Handling Deadlocks

We've just shown you how to handle the first two levels of problems that can occur, the impasse and the stalemate. If things get any worse, you may reach a deadlock, something that we define as, "Both sides are so frustrated with the lack of progress that they see no point in talking to each other any more."

Middle Negotiating Gambits

Deadlocks are rare, but if you do reach one, the *only* way to resolve it is to bring in a third party—someone who will act as a mediator or an arbitrator.

There is a major difference between an arbitrator and a mediator. In the case of binding arbitration, both sides agree before the process starts that they will abide by the arbitrator's decision. If a union that is critical to the public's welfare goes on strike, such as the transportation or sanitation workers' union, the federal government will eventually insist that an arbitrator be appointed, and both sides will have to settle for the solution that the arbitrator thinks is fair. With binding arbitration, there will be a winner and there will be a loser. Arbitration rarely comes into play in negotiating real estate deals unless the negotiation involves claims of deception, fraud, or other undesirable interactions between sellers and buyers or between buyers and lenders.

A mediator doesn't have that kind of power. A mediator is simply someone who is brought in to facilitate a solution. He or she simply acts as a catalyst, using his or her skills to seek a solution that both sides will accept as reasonable.

Let's say that you have signed a contract to buy a home, but your home inspection has revealed that the roof will soon need to be replaced. The seller is willing to give you a partial allowance for it, but not an entire new roof. He argues that the roof has five years of life left in it. Neither you nor the seller is inclined to spend any more time arguing about it. That's a deadlock that calls for a third-party mediator. Perhaps the broker who is in charge of handling the transaction for either the buyer or the seller will do. Roger is very familiar with this role. He would get the problems when his company's agents couldn't resolve them, the office managers couldn't resolve them either, and the regional managers had also failed. He was always amazed at how easily these problems could be resolved when a fresh face was introduced who positioned himself as neutral in the conflict. (A word here about resolving real estate conflict: it is easier to get the buyer to make concessions than to get the seller to do so. A $3,000 roof repair might mean a loss of $3,000 cash to the seller. It might mean only a $30 a month increase in payments to the buyer if you can get the lender to increase the buyer's loan.)

Inexperienced negotiators are reluctant to bring in a mediator because they see their inability to resolve a problem as being a failure on their part. What is running through the sales agent's mind is, "I don't want to ask my broker for help because she'll think that I'm a poor negotiator." Good negotiators know that there are many reasons why a third party can resolve a problem when they can't. It doesn't have to mean that the third party is a better negotiator.

Don't assume that you must avoid impasses, stalemates, and deadlocks at all costs. An experienced negotiator can use them as tools to pressure the other side. Once you have the mindset that a deadlock is unthinkable, this means that you're no longer willing to walk away, and you have surrendered your most powerful pressure point, as you'll see when we get to ending negotiating gambits.

Key Points to Remember

- The only way to resolve a true deadlock is by bringing in a third party.
- The third party can act as either a mediator or an arbitrator. Mediators can only facilitate a solution, but both sides agree up front that they will abide by an arbitrator's final decision.
- Don't view having to bring in a third person as a failure on your part. There are many reasons why third parties can reach a solution that the parties to the negotiation couldn't reach alone.
- The third party must be seen as neutral by both sides.
- Keep an open mind about the possibility of a deadlock. You can develop your full power as a negotiator only if you're willing to walk away. By refusing to consider a deadlock, you're giving away a valuable pressure point.
- You can learn more about the art of mediation and arbitration in Roger Dawson's book *Secrets of Power Negotiation* (Career Press).

Always Ask for a Trade-Off

The Trade-Off Gambit tells you that anytime the other side asks you for a concession in the negotiations, you should automatically ask for something in return. The first time you use this gambit, you'll get back the money you invested in this book many times over. From then on, using it will earn you thousands of dollars every year. Let's look at a couple of ways of using the Trade-Off Gambit:

- Let's say that you have bought a rental property, and the sellers ask you if they could leave some of their furniture in the garage for three days after the closing. That doesn't sound unreasonable to you, but remember the rule: however small the concession they're asking you for, always ask for something in return. Say to them, "Let me check with my partners (vague higher authority) and see how they feel about that, but let me ask you this: if we do that for you, what will you do for us?"

- Perhaps your agent calls you and tells you that the sellers need to delay the closing by a week. Although your initial inclination is to say, "That's fine," we still want you to use the Trade-Off Gambit. We want you to say, "Quite frankly, I don't know whether we can make that work. We have the painters scheduled to start work on the following Monday. I'll have to check with my property managers" (note again the use of a vague higher authority) "and see what they say about it. But let me ask you this, if we can do that for you, what can you do for us?"

One of three things is going to happen when you ask for something in return:

1. *You just might get something.* The buyers of your house may be willing to paint the kitchen or leave their patio furniture behind.
2. *By asking for something in return, you elevate the value of the concession.* When you're negotiating, why give anything away?

Always make a big deal out of it. You may need that later on for another trade-off. When you're doing the walkthrough with the buyers of the house, you may notice that the windows need to be cleaned. You're able to say, "Do you know how much it inconvenienced us to let you leave your furniture in the garage? We did that for you, and now I want you to pay for cleaning the windows." When you elevate the value of the concession, you set it up for a trade-off later.

3. *It stops the grinding-away process.* This is the key reason why you should always use the Trade-Off Gambit. If the negotiators on the other side know that every time they ask you for something, you're going to ask for something in return, then it stops them from constantly coming back for more. Many times a student of ours has come up to us at a seminar or gone into our chat room (at *www.weekendmillionaire.com*) and asked, "Can you help me with this? I thought I had a sweetheart of a deal put together. I didn't think that I would have any problems at all with this one. But in the very early stages, the sellers asked me for a small concession. I was so happy to be buying the property that I told them, 'Sure, we can do that.' A week later they called me for another small concession and I said: 'All right, I guess I can do that too.' Ever since then, it's been one darn thing after another. Now it looks as though the whole deal is going to fall apart on me." He should have known up front that when the other person asked him for that first small concession, he needed to ask for something in return. "If we can do that for you, what can you do for us?"

Please use these gambits word for word the way we're teaching them to you. If you change even a word, it can change the effect dramatically. If, for example, you change this from, "If we can do that for you, what can you do for us?" to "If we do that for you, you will have to do this for us," you have become confrontational. You've become confrontational at a very sensitive point in the negotiations—when the other side is under pressure and is asking you for a favor. Don't do it. It could cause the negotiation to blow up in your face.

You may be tempted to ask for a specific concession because you think you'll get more that way. We disagree. We think you'll get more by leaving the decision up to the other side. The value of whatever they offer reflects the value that they place on the concession they want you to make.

When you ask what they will give you in return, they may say, "Not a darn thing," or "You get to buy my property, that's what you get." That's fine, because you had everything to gain by asking, and you haven't lost anything. If necessary, you can always revert to a position of insisting on a trade-off by saying, "I don't think I can get my partners to agree to that unless you're willing to pick up the bill for doing this."

Key Points to Remember

- When the other side asks you for a small concession, always ask for something in return.
- Use this expression: "If we can do that for you, what can you do for us?"
- You may just get something in return.
- Doing this elevates the value of the concession so that you can use it as a trade-off later.
- Most important, it stops the grinding-away process.
- Don't change the wording by asking for something specific in return because it's too confrontational.

11

Ending Negotiating Gambits

As you get closer to reaching agreement with the seller, other factors come into play. In this chapter, we'll teach you the ending negotiating gambits that will bring the negotiations to a successful conclusion.

Nibbling

Good negotiators know that by using the Nibbling Gambit, you can get a little bit more even after you have agreed on everything. You can also get the other party to do things that he or she had refused to do earlier.

Car salespeople understand this, don't they? They know that when you come to the lot, you have built up a kind of psychological resistance to the purchase. First they get you to the point where you're thinking, "Yes, I'm going to buy a car. Yes, I'm going to buy it here." They do this even if it means closing you on a stripped-down make and model of car that carries little profit for them. Then they get you into the closing room and start adding all the other little extras that really build the profit into the car.

Nibbling tells you that you can accomplish some things more easily with a Nibble later in the negotiations.

Children are brilliant Nibblers, aren't they? If you have teenage children living at home, you know that they don't have to take any courses on negotiating. But you need to if you're going to stand a chance of surviving the whole process of bringing them up, because they're naturally brilliant negotiators. Not because they learn it in school, but because when they're little, everything they get, they get by negotiating.

When Roger's daughter Julia graduated from high school, she wanted to get a great high school graduation gift from her parents. She had three things on her negotiating agenda. Number one, she wanted a five-week trip to Europe. Number two, she wanted $1,200 in spending money. And number three, she wanted a new set of luggage.

She was smart enough not to ask for everything up front. She was a good enough negotiator to first close her parents on the trip, then come back a few weeks later, show them in writing that the recommended amount of spending money was $1,200, and get them to agree to that. Then, right at the last minute, she came to Roger and said, "Dad, you wouldn't want me going to Europe with that ratty old set of luggage, would you? All the kids will be there with new luggage." She got that, too. Had she asked for everything up front, he would have negotiated out the luggage and negotiated down the amount of spending money.

What's happening here is that a person's mind always works to reinforce decisions that it has just made. Our minds work to fight decisions right up until the time we make those decisions. Then the mind does a flip-flop and tends to do things that reinforce the decision that it just made. You need to know how this works and use it to get the sellers to agree to something that they wouldn't have agreed to earlier in the negotiation.

Why is Nibbling such an effective technique? To find out why this works so well, a couple of psychologists did a study at a racetrack in Canada. They studied the attitudes of people immediately before they placed a bet and again immediately after they had placed the bet. They found out that before the people placed the bet, they were uptight and unsure about what they were about to do. Compare this to a seller that you're trying to get to carry back financing: she may not know you, she may not know your character, and she certainly doesn't know what's going to come out of this relationship. Chances are that she's uptight, unsure, and anxious.

At the racetrack, the researchers found out that once people had made the decision to go ahead and place the bet, they suddenly felt good about what they had just done and even had a tendency to double the bet before the race started. In essence, their minds did a flip-flop once they had made the decision. Before they decided, they were fighting it; once they'd made the decision, they supported it.

If you're a gambler, you've had that sensation, haven't you? Watch gamblers at the roulette tables in Atlantic City or Vegas. They place their bets. The croupier spins the ball. At the very last moment, people are pushing out additional bets. The mind always works to reinforce decisions that it has made earlier.

Good negotiators don't necessarily ask for everything up front. They wait for a moment of agreement in the negotiations and then go back and Nibble for a little extra.

You might think of negotiating with a seller as pushing a ball uphill, a large rubber ball that's much bigger than you are. You're straining to force it up to the top of the hill. The top of the hill represents the moment of first agreement in the negotiations. Once you reach that point, then the ball moves easily down the other side of the hill. This is because people feel good after they have made the initial agreement. They feel a sense of relief that the tension and stress are over. Their minds are working to reinforce the decision that they've just made, and they're more receptive to any additional suggestions that you may have.

As a real estate investor, you may have trouble convincing the sellers that they should carry back financing, so you back off from the suggestion. After you have reached agreement on the other issues, however, you should have the courage to say, "Have you ever thought about creating an income stream from the equity in your property? If you cash out now, you'll have to pay taxes on the entire gain this year. If you create an income stream, you'll only pay taxes as you get the money. I don't recommend this for everybody, but for you it really makes sense. Why don't we take a look at setting it up that way?" You have a good chance of the seller saying, "All right, if you think it's that important, let's take another look at it."

Always go back at the end to make a second effort to get something that you couldn't get the seller to agree to earlier.

Look Out for People Nibbling on You

There's a point in the negotiation when you are very vulnerable to Nibbling, and that point is when you *think* the negotiations are over.

We bet you've been the victim of a Nibble at one time or another. You've been selling a car or a truck to someone. You're finally feeling good because you've found a buyer. The pressure and the tension of the negotiations have drained away. He's sitting in your office writing out the check. But just as he's about to sign his name, he looks up and says, "That does include a full tank of gas, doesn't it?"

You're at your most vulnerable point in the negotiations for two reasons:

1. You've just made a sale, and you're feeling good. When you feel good, you tend to give away things that you otherwise wouldn't.
2. You're thinking, "Oh, no. I thought we had resolved everything. I don't want to take a chance on having to go back to the

beginning and renegotiate the whole thing. If I do that, I might lose the entire sale. Perhaps I'm better off just giving in on this one little point."

You're at your most vulnerable just after the other person has made the decision to go ahead. Look out for people Nibbling on you. The seller has agreed to your proposal. She's reading your purchase offer, and she picks up her pen to sign it. At the last moment, she says, "By the way, you won't have a problem increasing the earnest money deposit to $10,000, will you?" Because you're excited about the deal and you're afraid to reopen the negotiations for fear of losing it, you'll have to fight to avoid the tendency to make the concession.

Countering the Nibble When the Other Person Does It to You

The counter gambit to the Nibble is to gently make the other person feel cheap. You have to be very careful about the way you do this because you're at a sensitive point in the negotiation. You smile sweetly and say, "Oh, come on, you negotiated a fantastic deal with me. Don't ask me to increase the earnest money, too. Fair enough?" Making the other person feel cheap is the counter gambit to the Nibble when it's used against you. Be sure that you do it with a big grin on your face, so that the other person doesn't take offense when you do it.

Consider these points when you go into negotiations:

- Are there some elements that you are better off bringing up as a Nibble after you have reached initial agreement?
- Do you have a plan to make a second effort when you can't get the other party to agree to certain things the first time around?
- Are you prepared for the possibility of the other party Nibbling on you at the last moment?

Great negotiators always take into account the possibility of being able to Nibble. Timing is very critical—catching the people on the other side when the tension is off and they're feeling good because they think the negotiations are all over.

On the other hand, look out for the other side Nibbling on you at the last moment, when you're feeling good. At that point, you're at your most vulnerable, and you're liable to make a concession that half an hour later you'll be thinking, "Why on earth did I do that? I didn't have to do that. We'd agreed on everything already."

Mike once used a Nibble to get a very expensive washer and dryer set that he was ultimately able to take home for his family's personal use. When he inspected the laundry room of a house on which he was planning to make a purchase offer, he noticed the brand-new appliances, with the energy efficiency stickers still on them. He thought, "Those are nicer than the ones I have at home. It would be nice if I could get the sellers to include them in the deal." He also assumed that since the sellers had obviously just purchased them, they probably wouldn't want to part with them when they sold their home, especially since he also planned to ask for the kitchen appliances in his initial offer.

What Mike did was make an offer that was far enough below the asking price to give him some negotiating room, but not so ridiculously low that it would offend the sellers. As he expected, the sellers countered his offer with a price reduction and a rejection of his request that they include the draperies and an antique rolltop desk. Mike countered with a corresponding increase in the price of his offer, but in doing so he made a big deal about wanting the desk and how he had put several thousand dollars into the offer to cover its value.

The negotiations went back and forth through several more offers and counteroffers until the sellers countered with a price and partial financing terms that were acceptable to Mike. Mike did not respond immediately to this offer, but waited until the seller's broker contacted him to see if he was going to accept the offer. At this point, Mike said, "I've been going over the offer and trying to see how I could make the numbers work. It's still about $3,000 more than what I feel I can pay, but I know we've all put a lot of time into trying to put the deal together. I'll tell you what, even though it's more than I want to pay, just to be fair, I'll go ahead with it if you can get your clients to throw in that washer and dryer set that was in the laundry room when I inspected the house." Within an hour, the broker called back to say that he had another copy of the seller's counteroffer with the washer and dryer included and to ask if he could bring it over to get Mike's signature on it.

Key Points to Remember

- With a well-timed Nibble, you can get things at the end of a negotiation that you couldn't have gotten from the other side earlier.
- The Nibble works because people's minds reverse themselves after they have made a decision. The people on the other side may have been fighting the thought of selling to you at the start of the negotiation. After they have made a decision to sell, however, you can Nibble for different terms and conditions that benefit you.
- Being willing to make that additional effort is what turns a great deal into a super deal.
- Stop the other person from Nibbling on you by not revealing that you have the authority to make any concessions.
- When the other person Nibbles on you, respond by making him or her feel cheap, in a good-natured way.

The Withdrawing the Offer Gambit

Walking away is the most important pressure point in negotiations. Suppose you said to us, "I don't have time to read your book now. I've got this appointment to meet with a motivated seller at noon today. Give me one thing that will make me a better negotiator!" Here's what we would tell you: "Power goes to the side that has convinced the other side that it is prepared to walk away from the negotiations if it can't get what it wants."

Let's say that a group of friends got together and bought a cabin in the mountains to use for a vacation home. There's a whole group of owners, and they're sharing the use of it. One partner drops out of the syndicate, and your neighbor, who is also a member, comes to you and tells you about the cabin in the mountains. Your initial reaction to this is, "This sounds fantastic. I'd love to do something like that." However, you're smart enough to use the Reluctant Buyer Gambit.

You say, "I appreciate your telling me about that, but I just don't think we'd be interested right now. I'm so busy that I don't think we'd have the time to get up there. But look, just to be fair to you, what is the very lowest price that you would sell a share in the home for?"

Your neighbor has been studying negotiating too, however, and he's learned that you should never be the first one to name the price. So he says, "We have a committee that decides on the price, and I don't know what that price would be. I can take them a proposal, but I don't know what the reaction would be."

When you press him a little more, he finally says, "I'm pretty sure that they're going to be asking $20,000."

This is a lot less than you expected. You were willing to go to $35,000. So your initial reaction is to jump at it right away, but you're smart enough to remember to Flinch. You exclaim, "$20,000. Oh, no, I could never go along with anything like that. That's way too much. Tell you what, $18,000 might interest me. If they're interested at $18,000, let me know and we'll talk about it."

The next day he comes back, and he has decided to bring you into line by using the Withdrawing the Offer Gambit. He says, "Am I embarrassed about this. I know that we were talking $20,000 yesterday, but the committee decided last night that it wouldn't sell a share for less than $25,000."

This is psychologically devastating to you for two reasons:

Ending Negotiating Gambits

1. You feel that you created the problem—you say, "Boy, I wish I'd never tried negotiating with them because if I hadn't, I would have nailed him down at $20,000 yesterday."

2. You've made the mistake of telling your family all about it. They're all excited about the home up in the mountains, and you've passed that critical point in the negotiations when you're prepared to walk away.

You say, "Joe, what are you talking about? You said $20,000 yesterday, and now it's $25,000 today; is it going to be $35,000 tomorrow? What's going on here?"

He says, "I do feel bad, but that's what they" (Higher Authority) "decided."

You say, "Joe, come on."

Joe says, "Well, I do feel bad about this. Tell you what, let me go back to them one more time, let me see what I can do for you with them. If I can get it for you for the $20,000, are you interested?"

And you say, "Of course I'm interested. I want it!" He has sold you at full price, and you may not realize what he's done until later.

Haven't we all had an appliance or car salesperson, when we were trying to force the price a little lower, say, "Let me go to my sales manager, and I'll see what I can do for you with him"? Then he comes back and says, "Am I embarrassed about this. You know that advertised special we were talking about? I thought that ad was still in effect, but it went off last Saturday. I can't even sell it to you at the price we were talking about."

Immediately you forget future concessions and want to jump on the bandwagon at the price you'd been talking about.

The Withdrawing an Offer Gambit is a gamble, but it will force a decision and will usually make or break the deal. Whenever the other person uses this on you, don't be afraid to counter by insisting that the other side resolve its internal problem first, so that you can then resume the real negotiation.

> ### Key Points to Remember
>
> - Withdrawing an Offer is a gamble, so use it only on someone who is grinding away on you.
> - You can do this by backing off your last price concession or by withdrawing an offer to sweeten the terms.
> - To avoid direct confrontation, make the bad guy a vague Higher Authority. Continue to position yourself as being on the other person's side.

How to Taper Concessions

In extended negotiations over price, be careful that you don't set up a pattern in the way you make concessions. Let's say that you're buying a rental property and you've gone into the negotiation with a price of $150,000, but you could still make the numbers work at $160,000. You have a negotiating range of $10,000. The way in which you concede that $10,000 is very critical. There are several mistakes that you should avoid:

Making equal-sized concessions. This means giving away your $10,000 negotiating range in four increments of $2,500 each. Imagine what the sellers are thinking if you do that. They don't know how far they can push you because all they know is that every time they push, they get another $2,500. They're going to keep on pushing. In fact, it's a mistake to make any two concessions of equal size. If you were buying a house and the owners made a $2,500 concession and then, when pushed, made another $2,500 concession, wouldn't you bet that the next concession would also be $2,500?

Making the final concession a big one. Let's say that you made a $6,000 concession followed by a $4,000 concession. Then you tell the other person, "That's absolutely our bottom line. I can't give you a penny more." The problem is that $4,000 is too big a concession to be your final concession. The other person is probably thinking that you made a $6,000 concession, followed by a $4,000 concession, so he's sure that he can get at least another $1,000 out of you. He says, "We're getting close. If you can come up another $1,000, we can talk." You refuse, telling him that you can't come up even another $100, because you've given him your bottom line already. By now the other person is really upset, because he's thinking, "You just made a $4,000 concession and now you won't give me another lousy $1,000. Why are you being so difficult?" Avoid making the last concession a big one, because it creates hostility.

Giving it all away up front. Another variation of the pattern is to give the entire $10,000 negotiating range away in one concession. When we set this up as a workshop at our seminars, it's amazing to us how many participants will turn to the person with whom they're to negotiate and say, "Well, I'll tell you what he told me." Such naiveté is a disastrous way to negotiate. We call it Unilateral Disarmament. Unilateral Disarmament is the seller who says to you, "I don't like to negotiate. I don't think that it's the fair way to conduct business. You just give me your very best price, and I'll tell you whether I'll accept it or not, because I don't like to negotiate." He is lying to you. He loves negotiating! That is negotiating—seeing if you can get the other person to make all of his or her concessions up front.

You may be thinking, "How would a person be able to get me to do a stupid thing like that?" It's easy. Someone who looked at the car you're trying to sell yesterday calls you up and says, "We've located three cars that we like equally well, so now we're just down to price. We thought the fairest thing to do would be to let all three sellers give us their very lowest price, so that we can decide." Unless you're a skilled negotiator, you'll panic and cut your price to the bone, although the buyer hasn't given you any assurance that there won't be another round of bidding later.

Giving a small concession to test the waters. Giving a small concession first to see what happens is tempting for all of us. You initially tell the sellers, "I might be able to go up another $1,000, but that's our limit." If the sellers reject that, you might think, "This isn't going to be as easy as I thought." So you offer another $2,000. That still doesn't get them to sell you the property, so in the next round you give away another $3,000, and then you have $4,000 left in your negotiating range, so you give them the whole thing.

You see what you've done there? You started with a small concession and built up to a larger concession. You'll never reach agreement doing that, because every time the other party asks you for a concession, it just gets better and better for him or her.

All of these scenarios are wrong because they create a pattern of expectations in the other person's mind. The best way to make concessions is to start by offering a reasonable concession that just might cinch the deal. Maybe a $4,000 concession wouldn't be out of line. Then be sure that if you have to make any further concessions, they're smaller and smaller. Your next concession might be $3,000, and then $2,000, and then $1,000. By reducing the size of the concessions that you're making, you convince the other person that he or she has pushed you about as far as you will go.

If you want to see how effective this can be, try it on your children. Wait until the next time they come to you for money for a school outing. They ask you for $100. You say, "No way. Do you realize that when I was your age, my weekly allowance was 50 cents? Out of that, I had to buy my own shoes and walk 10 miles to school in the snow, uphill both ways. I would take my shoes off and walk barefoot to save money." (Or one of the other stories that parents the world over tell their children.) "No way am I going to give you $100. I'll give you $50 and that's it."

"I can't do it on $50," your children protest in horror.

Now you have established the negotiating range. They are asking for $100. You're offering $50. The negotiations progress at a frenzied pace, and you move up to $60. Then you go to $65 and finally to $67.50." By the time you've reached $67.50, you don't have to tell them that they're not going to do any better. By tapering your concessions, you have subliminally communicated that fact.

This pattern works equally well whether you're negotiating with your children over $50 or negotiating a $50 million real estate deal. By making each concession smaller, you are telling the other side that it is getting closer and closer to the maximum concession that you are willing to make.

Key Points to Remember

- The way in which you make concessions can create a pattern of expectations in the seller's mind.
- Don't make equal-size concessions because the sellers will keep on pushing.
- Don't make your last concession a big one because it creates hostility.
- Never concede your entire negotiating range just because the sellers call for your "last and final" proposal or claim that they "don't like to negotiate."
- Taper the concessions to communicate to the other side that it is getting the best possible deal.

Positioning for Easy Acceptance

The Positioning for Easy Acceptance Gambit is very important, particularly if you're dealing with sellers who have studied negotiating. If they're proud of their ability to negotiate, even when you get ridiculously close to agreement, the entire negotiation can still fall apart.

When it does, it's probably not the price or terms of the agreement that caused the problem; it's the ego of the other person as a negotiator.

You have another appointment with a couple who turned down your offer last month. You're hopeful that they haven't had a better offer and that they are now willing to accept your proposal. What you may not realize is that just before you showed up in their home, the husband said to his wife, "You just watch me negotiate with this investor. I know what I'm doing, and I'll get us a good price."

Now you've been negotiating for a couple of hours, and he's not doing as well as he'd hoped. He's reluctant to agree to your proposal because he doesn't want to feel that he lost to you as a negotiator. This can happen even when the other person knows that your proposal is fair and that it satisfies his needs in every way.

When this happens, you must find a way to make the other person feel good about giving in to you. You must Position for Easy Acceptance. The best way to do this is to make a small concession just at the last moment. Even if the size of the concession is ridiculously small, you can still make this gambit work because it's not the size of the concession that's critical, but the timing.

You might say, "We just can't budge on the price, but I tell you what. If you'll go along with the price, I'll agree to move the closing date up 15 days."

Perhaps that's a minor concession to you, but the point is that you've been courteous enough to position the seller so that he can respond, "Well, all right, if you'll do that for me, we'll go along with the price." That lets him feel that he didn't lose in the negotiation. What he did was conclude it by getting you to trade off for something that benefited him, even if it was insignificant in the overall transaction.

Mike encountered a situation like this once when he was negotiating to purchase a house and asking for seller financing. Mike started out asking the sellers to finance most of the purchase at 0 percent interest for 15 years. The sellers counteroffered to accept his price, but they wanted 8 percent interest on the loan. Mike countered with another offer at 8 percent interest, but at a substantially lower price. Both sides made several concessions in both price and interest rate, and finally the negotiations had reached a point where Mike offered a price that was acceptable to the sellers, with them financing the purchase at 4.5 percent interest.

The wife, who had been silent throughout, finally said, "Why don't we just go ahead and take his offer and get rid of the house?" To which the husband responded, "I'd be willing to take it if he would come up to 5 percent interest, but not a bit less at that price."

Here Mike used the Positioning for Easy Acceptance Gambit by calmly saying, "You have negotiated a fantastic deal, but I simply can't give any more. I really want to make this deal, but the only way I could pay 5 percent interest would be to cut the price some more, and I don't think you are willing to do that. How about if I do something else instead? If you will agree to accept my offer, I will remove the old roof shingles and replace them with new 30-year architectural shingles." (This was something that he planned to do anyway.) "This will improve the value of the house and give you even better security for the purchase money loan."

The husband immediately said, "That's fair enough." Then he turned to his wife and said, "Isn't that great? I was afraid he was going to ask us to replace the roof." What he didn't know was that Mike had already factored the cost of replacing the roof into his offer; he just hadn't mentioned it to them. By offering to replace the roof, Mike had given the husband a way to look good in his wife's eyes without having to make any further concessions in price or terms.

Positioning for Easy Acceptance is another reason why you should never go in with your best offer up front. If you have offered all of your concessions before you get to the end of the negotiation, you won't have anything left with which to position the other side.

The concession can be ridiculously small and still be effective. By using this gambit, you can make the other person feel good about giving in.

Key Points to Remember

- If the other person is proud of his or her ability to negotiate, his or her egotistical need to win may stop you from reaching agreement.
- Position the other person to feel good about giving in to you by making a small concession at the last moment.
- Because timing is more important than the size of the concession, the concession can be ridiculously small and still be effective.

12

Negotiating with People from Foreign Cultures

That America is a land of immigrants is an expression that has remained true since the pilgrims landed on Plymouth Rock. In many major cities, you are in a minority if both of your parents were born in this country. This means that it won't be very long before you're negotiating a real estate transaction with someone who thinks like a foreigner.

In this brief look at the topic (there's much more in Roger's book *Secrets of Power Negotiating*), we'll talk about how Americans negotiate and where we get into problems when we're dealing with people from other cultures.

Americans Focus on the Deal

New York real estate investor Donald Trump wrote a bestselling book, *The Art of the Deal,* that detailed many of his early real estate negotiations. The title and the premise of the book illuminate the overriding concern of most American negotiators—cutting the deal. We live in a very deal-conscious environment.

We suppose sociologists would tell you that we concentrate more on making the deal than people from other nations do because we are such a mobile and diverse society with little sense of roots. Instead of trusting the people around us and the way things are done, as is common elsewhere in the world, we put all of our effort into creating an unbreakable deal. "Will it hold up in court?" we demand, as though anyone who doesn't consider the possibility of having to defend the deal in court is naive. In America, all real estate contracts must be in writing if they are to hold up in court.

Most foreigners completely reject our dependence on the deal. If they choose to sign a contract at all, it is simply an expression of an understanding that existed on a particular date. It is a formal expression of the relationship that now exists between the parties. And like any other relationship, it must mold itself to changing conditions.

Most Americans are astounded to learn that you can sign a contract in Korea and have it mean nothing six months later. "But we signed a contract," the Americans howl.

"Yes," their Korean counterpart patiently explains, "we signed a contract based on the conditions that existed six months ago when we signed it. Those conditions no longer exist, so the contract we signed is meaningless."

"Foul!" cries the American. "You are trying to cheat me." Not at all. What seems to us to be a disreputable action does not seem like one to them, and we should not attempt to paint it as such. It is merely their way of doing things.

Americans are often delighted to find that they had little trouble getting their Arabian trading partners to sign a contract. Then they are horrified to find out that in the Arab world, signing the contract announces the start of the negotiations, not the end. A signed contract means less in their culture than a letter of intent does in ours. We are not putting this down, and neither should you. What you should do is recognize that different nationalities and different cultures have different ways of doing things, and that it behooves you to learn, understand, and appreciate those different ways.

It will come as no surprise to you to learn that Americans resort to legal action more quickly and more frequently than any other people on earth. Our readiness to resort to legal action would be laughable to a businessman in India, where the civil legal system is close to nonexistent. It would take you five years to have a civil case heard there, and most realistic people would suggest that you forget it because it's questionable whether the system will even be functioning five years from now. Even the chief justice of India has said in public that the system is about to collapse. Indians must rely on their faith in the person with whom they are doing business.

In America, legal action is so common that companies continue to do business with a company that is suing them. We see legal action as a normal way to resolve a dispute and no reason for animosity. In most foreign countries, there is such a loss of face involved in being sued by another company that companies will refuse to deal in any way with a company that is suing them.

Here we have the essence of how the way Americans think about negotiating differs from that of people from other cultures. We think of negotiating as doing what is needed to get the other side to sign a contract. The faster we can get it done, the better. This is one of the reasons why we are reluctant to make outrageous demands. We see making such demands as slowing down the process. Asians have no trouble making outrageous demands because they assume that the negotiations will take weeks or months and there will be plenty of time for each side to make concessions until an agreement is reached.

The first thing we should learn about negotiating with foreigners is that the deal is not the major issue to them. They put far more trust in the relationship between the parties. Is there good blood between the parties? If there is only bad blood, no amount of legal maneuvering will make the relationship worthwhile. While you are trying to hammer out the fine points of the deal, they are spending their time assessing the fine points of your character.

Getting Down to Business with Foreigners

Now let's talk about the other major mistake that we Americans make in dealing with foreigners—we want to get down to business too quickly.

Nobody gets down to business faster than Americans do. Typically, we exchange a few pleasantries to ease any tension and then get right down to hammering out the details of the deal. We socialize afterward. Foreigners may take days, weeks, or even months before they feel comfortable moving from the getting-to-know-you stage to the point where they feel good about doing business with you.

When the Shah of Iran fell from power, the Los Angeles real estate company of which Roger was president did a huge amount of business with Iranians (they prefer to be called Persians) who were fleeing the new regime, often with millions of dollars in cash to invest. He watched his salespeople make the mistake of trying to talk business too soon, which caused the Iranians to distrust them. Many of the problems went away when the salespeople learned that Persians wanted to sit and drink tea for several hours while they sized up the agent and the company.

When negotiating with foreigners, we Americans will do much better if we slow down. We tend to speak first, then listen to the response, and only then observe the behavior of the other negotiators. Foreigners tell us that we should reverse that order. We should observe first, then listen, and finally speak. In fact, reacting slowly to the other side's proposal is a mark of respect. Your silence does not indicate acceptance of the proposal; it merely indicates that you are giving the proposal the consideration it deserves.

As we have seen, Americans fall into two major traps when dealing with foreigners: we emphasize the deal over the importance of the relationship between the parties, and we get down to business too quickly. The two are closely related, of course. Building a relationship with the other side to the point where you feel comfortable with him or her takes time. Enlarging on that relationship to the point where you trust the other person and don't have to rely on the contract being airtight takes a great deal of time.

How Different Cultures Negotiate Differently

Let's take a look at some of the differences between the way we Americans negotiate and the way people from foreign cultures do so.

> *We tend to be very direct in our communications.* Americans use expressions such as "What's your bottom line?" or "How much profit would you make at that figure?" Or we try to shift the emphasis of the negotiations by saying things like, "Let's lay our cards on the table," or "Let's wrap this one up tonight." We "tell it like it is," "shoot from the hip," and try to "hit the nail on the head." We seldom "beat around the bush." Although we recommend this kind of directness when negotiating with other Americans because it puts pressure on the other side, you need to realize that it may seem too abrupt to foreigners, and that such bluntness may offend them.
>
> *We resist making outrageous initial demands.* This goes back to our hope that we can cut the deal and "get out of Dodge." Because we want to blitz the negotiations and wrap them up quickly, we tend to think in much shorter time frames than foreigners do. We're thinking that we can conclude the negotiations in hours, while they're thinking that the process will take many days. Although foreigners may be comfortable making an outrageous initial demand because they know that the price and terms will change enormously as the days go by, we see this as slowing the negotiations down or drawing us into endless haggling.

We are more likely to negotiate alone. It's not unusual to find a lone American negotiator who is fully empowered to do business showing up at an international negotiation. When he is led into the negotiating room, he finds that he is faced with a team of 10 or 12 people from the other side. This is not good for the American, because he will feel psychologically overwhelmed unless the negotiating teams are roughly the same size. However, the effect of this on the foreign team concerns us more. Foreigners may interpret the sending of a lone negotiator as meaning, "They're not serious about making a deal at this meeting, because if they've only sent one negotiator, this must be only a preliminary expedition." Or foreigners may get the impression that the American is merely gathering information to take back to a team of negotiators. Unless the American understands this and takes pains to explain that he is the entire negotiating team and that he is empowered to negotiate the deal, he may not be taken seriously. This puts him at a serious disadvantage because it removes his ability to resort to Higher Authority. If he is forced to emphasize his authority to negotiate, he should point out that he has the authority to negotiate only up to a certain price point. Beyond that point, he will need to get authorization. If pressed to reveal that price point, he should explain that he is not empowered to do so.

Americans are uncomfortable with emotional displays. The English are the most uncomfortable with them, of course, but Americans also see displaying emotions in public as a weakness. If an American wife starts to cry, her husband instantly assumes that he has done something devastatingly cruel to her. In the Mediterranean countries, the husband simply wonders what ploy his wife has concocted now. This fear of an emotional reaction causes Americans to be tentative in their negotiations with foreigners, and if the seller does explode with anger at one of our low offers, we tend to overreact. Instead, we should merely see this as a negotiating ploy that might be perfectly acceptable in another culture.

We are uncomfortable with silence. Americans hate silence. To us, 15 seconds of silence seems like an eternity. Do you remember the last time the high-definition picture broke up on your plasma television? You were probably thumping the top of the set within 15 seconds. Particularly to Asians, who are comfortable with long periods of meditation, this impatience appears to be a weakness that they can take advantage of. When dealing with foreigners, don't be intimidated by long periods of silence. See it as a challenge not to be the next one to talk. After an extended period of silence, the next person to talk loses. The next person to open his or her mouth will make a concession. One of Roger's students, a mortgage banker, told a story of negotiating in Shanghai, China. "There were 20 of us around a conference table," he told Roger. "Tens of millions of dollars in mortgages were at stake. Suddenly the other side went completely quiet. Fortunately, I had learned about this tactic and was prepared for it. I glanced at my watch. A full 33 minutes went by without a word being spoken. Finally one of their lawyers spoke up and made a concession that enabled us to put the transaction together."

We hate to admit that we don't know. Americans hate to admit that they don't know. This is something that foreigners realize and can use to their advantage. You don't have to answer every question. You are perfectly entitled to say, "That's privileged information at this stage." Or you can simply tell them that you don't know or that you are not permitted to release the information they seek. Not every question deserves an answer.

There's an old joke that the restaurants in heaven have a German manager, a French maître d', English waiters, and an Italian cook. On the other hand, the restaurants in hell have an Italian manager, a German maître d', French waiters, and an English cook. These are stereotypes, sure, but it would be wrong to ignore ethnic and national business characteristics in the name of avoiding any stereotyping.

We would be guilty of stereotyping if we implied that all people from these countries or with these national backgrounds have the tendencies we've discussed here. However, it's realistic to assume that a large percentage of immigrants behave this way. You'll be much more successful in dealing with people from other cultures if you keep these characteristics in mind.

When Mike was in the advertising business, he encountered nearly all of these negotiating styles because many of his clients owned ethnic restaurants. He quickly learned that selling advertising to the owners or managers of Chinese, Japanese, Indian, Greek, Italian, and Mexican restaurants was totally different from dealing with Joe down at the Good Ol' Boy Café. The experience that Mike gained working with people from different cultures has served him well in his real estate venture. He has successfully made purchases from Greek and Chinese sellers whose negotiating tactics turned off other potential buyers.

Key Points to Remember from This Chapter

- Americans focus more on getting the contract signed than on building a relationship with the other person.
- Americans want to get down to business too quickly.
- We tend to be very direct in our communications.
- We resist making outrageous initial demands, thinking that doing so will slow down the negotiation.
- We are more likely to negotiate alone.
- We are uncomfortable with emotional displays.
- We are uncomfortable with silence.
- We hate to admit that we don't know.

13

Understanding Sellers' Personality Styles

I n this chapter, we're going to teach you how to analyze sellers' personality styles and how to use that information to adapt your negotiating style to better fit theirs. Knowing the differing personality styles will help you get a better deal and make the entire negotiating process more agreeable for everyone.

Personality styles develop very early in life. The Jesuits used to say, "Give me a child until he is seven, and we will give you the man," which is based on a quote by the Spanish saint Francis Xavier. If you've raised children, you know about that, don't you? It's one of life's little mysteries how children who are raised together in exactly the same circumstances can grow up completely different from one another. If you look back to when they were just seven years old, you will see that they had the same personality styles then that they have today as adults.

The system we're going to teach you is based on something that the Greek philosopher Hippocrates worked out a couple of thousand years ago, so it is time-tested and proven.

The system is based on two dimensions. The first dimension is the seller's assertiveness level. You can tell this by the firmness of the seller's handshake, the directness of his or her responses to your questions, and whether he or she volunteered his or her name easily when shaking your hand—that kind of thing. The assertive seller wants to get down to business quickly. He or she will shake hands and say, "Come on in and let's see if this property will work for you." An unassertive person wants to take the time to get to know you. An assertive buyer will make a decision quickly: "Your offer looks fine except for the price. I need to get $20,000 more." The unassertive buyer wants time to think it over or refer it to a partner.

Assertive people are always eager to sell their ideas and philosophies to other people, so they are typically persuaders. They're always trying to talk people into buying the same kind of car they drive or moving to the part of town they favor.

Assertive people have short attention spans. Their minds are constantly jumping from one thing to another. They're thinking of all the phone calls they have to make and all the things they have to do. Because they know they won't be thinking about the same thing five minutes from now, they get into the habit of making decisions quickly. They'll look at your offer and either go for it or not go for it quickly.

Less assertive people have long attention spans, so they get into the habit of making decisions slowly—they genuinely need time to think things over.

Recognize this as a major point of conflict in getting the seller to accept your offer. If you're a fast decision maker, the less assertive slow decision makers can drive you up the wall. You'll be thinking, "He's had my offer for three days now. I call him up, and he says he's still thinking about it! For heaven's sake, how long does it take anybody to make up his mind? It's only $300,000. It's not that big a deal."

If you're an unassertive person, you're probably a slow decision maker, and you're very suspicious of fast decision makers.

You say, "I took the offer in to this buyer, and she looked at it briefly, it couldn't have been more than a minute, and said, 'I'll take it if you'll raise your price by $10,000.' I don't think she took my offer seriously. It's just not natural for people to make decisions that quickly."

The second dimension is the seller's emotional level. This is the same as the left-brain versus right-brain way of thinking. Emotional, or right-brain, people are creative and care about people. Unemotional, or left-brain, people see things in black and white and care about facts, not feelings. Evaluate the way the seller describes the home and the warmth with which he or she responds to people. Emotional sellers care about what happens to the property after they sell. They want to know that the buyer will love the home as much as they have. Unemotional sellers care only about whether or not you can get the financing and whether your deposit check will clear the bank.

Let's look at these dimensions on a chart:

	Low ASSERTIVENESS	High
Low EMOTION	Low Emotion Low Assertive	Low Emotion High Assertive
High	High Emotion Low Assertive	High Emotion High Assertive

Now let's identify your personality on this chart. To do this, we ask you to assume that you've just completed one of our Weekend Millionaire seminars. We'll place you on the chart based on your reaction to the all-day seminar. We'll start in the top right-hand corner and go around clockwise.

Pragmatics

People with an assertive-unemotional personality, found in the top right-hand corner, will sit through an all-day seminar for one reason and one reason only: they want to learn. They're not going to stay because they like the speaker or because they are having a good time. They are interested only in the amount of useful information with which they can leave the room. The speaker can use a little humor, but only if it's relevant. "I didn't come here to listen to a bunch of jokes," they're thinking.

Pragmatics are surrounded by time-management gadgets. Anything that they can get that will make them more efficient, they will have. Laptops, BlackBerries, GPSs, iPhones—they've got them all. They hate wasting time. If you're married to a Pragmatic, you'll see your spouse go into the living room to watch the evening news and then say, "Darn it, I'm here a minute and a half early. What am I going to do with the time? I can't waste it!" Then he or she will get the remote control and go through 40 channels of cable in a minute and a half and do the same thing during commercials. TiVo is heaven-sent to Pragmatics. They have figured out that they can watch a 30-minute television program in 22 minutes and 12 seconds by fast-forwarding through the commercials.

The other thing that Pragmatics think is a total waste of time is going on vacation. If you're married to a Pragmatic, you know how hard it is to get your spouse to go in the first place. Don't drag Pragmatics off to a place where there is nothing to do but sit on the beach. They can't take much of that. By the end of the second day, they're getting bored. By the third day, they'll be organizing something like a volleyball championship or a bridge tournament.

The Pragmatic is a down-to-earth, no-nonsense businessperson. Pragmatic sellers are interested only in the basics. How much are you going to give them for their property, and how are they going to get it? Will your deposit check clear the bank, and can you get the financing? They don't care what you're going to do with the property, and they don't care who will be living there after they leave.

It will help you to identify Pragmatics to realize that they don't like spectator sports. The thought of sitting in a stadium for three hours, watching someone else do something, is not for them. They like active sports where they can be out there doing it themselves.

Extroverts

Extroverts, in the bottom right-hand corner of the chart, will only sit through to the end of an all-day seminar because they are enjoying it. Unlike the Pragmatic, they love spectator sports. The thought of being in that stadium with all those cheering people is about as good as life gets for them. Remember that these are assertive, emotional people. They fall in love with things. Real estate salespeople save their curb-appeal properties for buyers of this type. Curb appeal refers to what the property looks like when you first pull up out front. If it looks like Tara from *Gone with the Wind*, with the big columns in front, the big visual appeal, these people fall in love with the property; they want it, and they want it right now. They tend to behave the same way at cocktail parties, too. They want to be the center of attention, and they will often do things like getting up and dancing by themselves in order to be seen. They don't like to be alone, and they are crushed by criticism, even when it is justified. They seek the acceptance and approval of others and may discuss your offers with people who have no interest in the transaction just to feel that someone else agrees with the decision they are about to make.

The Swiss psychiatrist Carl G. Jung defined extroversion as turning the interests and energies of the mind toward events, people, and things in the world about us. Extroverts, he pointed out, are more interested in what is going on around them than in their own thoughts and feelings.

Amiables

Amiables, in the bottom left-hand corner of the chart, are emotional, like Extroverts, but nonassertive. They will sit through an all-day seminar because they don't want to offend the speaker by leaving early. Amiables tend to set up barriers. They probably have an unlisted home phone number, and they may have a "No Peddlers" sign on the front door because they hate high pressure. They have probably lived in the same home for a long time because they develop relationships with things as well as with people.

An Amiable drives an older car because he or she fears going to a dealer and being ground to death by a high-pressure salesperson. Amiables are not entrepreneurs. If they are trying to sell a property themselves, they will quickly get discouraged and list it with a broker. They have a poor sense of time management. If you call and ask an Amiable for an appointment to see the property, he or she is likely to tell you to drop by any time. Amiables tend to be disorganized because they can't say no to people. Their environment is warm and comfortable because they form relationships with the things in their life, such as homes, furniture, and cars, and don't like to change them. Amiables care about who lives in the property after they have moved. They want the tenant to love the property as much as they have. An Amiable may not even want to sell the property to you if he or she thinks that you are going to turn the home into a rental unit.

When you're dealing with an Amiable, go slowly. Build trust before getting down to business. Demonstrate that you really care about people. Be careful, because the slightest little thing may offend this type of person. Don't high-pressure him or her because an Amiable doesn't like being forced into making a decision. You'll just have to accept that and give the Amiable time to think things through, because you aren't going to get a decision until the Amiable feels comfortable with you.

Analyticals

The fourth personality style (in the top left-hand corner of the chart) is the unassertive-unemotional person that we call the Analytical. He or she will sit through an all-day seminar to be sure that they got and understood all the details. The Analytical will often have a background in engineering or accounting. He or she probably has gadget mania and is surrounded by computers, calculators, and iPods; the Analytical was the first person in the state to have an iPhone on his or her belt at all times. Analyticals are very curious people who soak up information and can't get enough of it. Show them a book and they'll want to know when and how it was printed.

Analyticals feel that they can manage everything just by generating massive amounts of information. They are very precise about punctuality, so when you call for an appointment to view the property, they won't say, "Come around lunchtime." They are more likely to say, "Can you be here at ten after one?"

Analyticals are also very precise about figures, so they won't tell you that the new door on the house cost them over seven hundred dollars. They'll tell you that it cost $714.16.

With the Analytical, you need to be accurate. Ask an Analytical what day of the week it is, and he or she will tell you, "It's Wednesday. Except on the island of Guam, where it's already Thursday morning." The Analytical is fascinated by analysis and has charts and graphs for everything. When such a person asks you for figures, give them to the penny. Be prepared to provide every little detail of the offer. Try to build rapport with the Analytical by talking about topics that interest him or her, which probably include engineering and computer technology.

The Seller Who Will Give You the Most Problems

You should recognize that you will have the most difficulty with people with the personality style that is in the opposite corner from yours on the chart—the one that is opposite on both the assertive and the emotional dimension. Let's take a look again at the quadrants with the personalities added:

If you are an assertive-unemotional Pragmatic (in the top right-hand quarter), you love dealing with other Pragmatics. They are down-to-earth, no-nonsense sellers, and if you ask them a question, you'll get an answer. When you want a decision, you'll get it, and they'll live with it. It's when you have to deal with the unassertive-emotional Amiables that you run into difficulty. You're thinking quickly and unemotionally, but they're thinking slowly and emotionally.

You'll take an offer to an Amiable, and you don't see any reason in the world why he or she shouldn't go along with it. It's clear to you that your offer is a good deal. The sellers ought to jump at it, but they are holding back. They're probably thinking, "I don't feel comfortable with you yet, and I'm not going to sell my property to you until I do. Don't tell me how much you know until you tell me how much you care."

Conversely, the Amiable seller will have the most difficulty with Pragmatics such as you. You seem so hardheaded and impersonal to an Amiable. You seem to be all business, with no feeling for people. The Amiable needs time to feel good about doing business with you.

If you're an assertive-emotional Extrovert, you love other Extroverts. They're fun people who will go off and do exciting things at the drop of a hat. It's when you have to deal with the unassertive-unemotional Analytical that you run into difficulties. To you, Analyticals always seem to need too much information. They're too much into the details and don't seem able to see the big picture. You see them as far too cautious in the way they do things because accuracy is next to Godliness to an Analytical.

When an Analytical says to you, "When will you close the deal?" she wants to hear you say, "On January 16 by 3:15 in the afternoon." She doesn't want to hear, "Oh, about the middle of January or so." She wants to hear it out to the minute.

Conversely, the Analytical thinks that you as an Extrovert are too flippant. You're too easygoing, and you go off on different tangents without really having all the information that you ought to have about the situation. If you're too quick to make an offer on the property, the Analytical will view this as confirmation that you are too flippant and won't trust you. He wants to feel that you have at least given the appearance of having put considerable thought into preparing your offer.

People with Different Personality Styles Negotiate Differently

The reason that you need to understand these personality styles is that people with each of them negotiate differently. If you can identify the personality style of the sellers you will be dealing with, you'll get a good feeling about how they will attempt to negotiate with you.

The Pragmatic

In a negotiation situation, the Pragmatic turns into a Street Fighter. A Street Fighter's only goal in the negotiation is to win, and to him or her, winning means that somebody else has to lose, and what's wrong with that? "That's the way the world is—don't waste my time with all this wishy-washy win-win nonsense. Why on earth would I be concerned about the other party's needs in the negotiations? That's their job! I expect them to fight as hard for what they want as I'm going to fight for what I want."

You would think that a Street Fighter would be the type that you'd least like to buy a property from, but Street Fighters have a vulnerable flaw. That flaw is that they become obsessed with one issue in the negotiation. This is because they see negotiating as a game to be won or lost, and they must have a way to score the game. The seller who is a Street Fighter may decide that winning the negotiation with you means that he gets $200,000 for his property. He will become obsessed with that one issue, but if you realize this, you'll find that he will give away everything else in order to achieve that goal.

Let's say that you are dealing with a Street Fighter seller who has made up his mind that he won't take a penny less than $200,000 for his property. If you take him an offer at $195,000, he will turn it down because if he accepted it, he would feel that he had lost. However, if you take him an offer at $200,000 that asks him to carry back a $50,000 note with 6 percent interest added, due and payable in 10 years, he will accept it. It is a worse offer than the $195,000 cash-out offer if you consider the time value of money, but he will turn that down because it doesn't meet the criteria by which he's scoring the game. If you really want to win over the Street Fighter, grudgingly take him an offer for $210,000 that asks him to finance the purchase at 3 percent interest. He'll probably accept it and tell all his friends that he got $10,000 more than he was asking for his property, without ever mentioning the low-rate financing that he provided.

Another thing about the Street Fighter is that in order for him to feel that he won, he must see that someone else is losing. Don't talk win-win to a Street Fighter. Instead, bleed over him and tell him how much you're hurting.

The Extrovert

The Extrovert turns into a Den Mother as a negotiator. A Den Mother is someone who gets so excited about things that she tends to lose perspective. This is the person who is organizing a softball team at work, and she's so excited and enthusiastic about it! It doesn't occur to her that there's anybody in the entire world who wouldn't want to play softball on Tuesday evenings.

Den Mothers are the people who are most likely to have the whole negotiation fall down around them before they realize that there is a problem. This is the real estate agent who comes back into his office and kicks the desk. "My buyers bought from another broker! How could they do this to me? I was out drinking with them until midnight the other night." Den Mothers let their enthusiasm blind them to the reality of the situation.

The Amiable

The Amiable tends to turn into a Pacifier as a negotiator. The Pacifier's objective in the negotiations is not so much to win as to see that everybody is happy. It's interesting to see the opposite personality style, the Street Fighter, negotiating with the Pacifier. The Street Fighter will try to grind every last dime out of the negotiations until she's convinced that there's not another penny left on the table, and when it's all over, the Pacifier will turn to her and say, "Now are you sure this is fair? I wouldn't want to take advantage of you."

The Analytical

The Analytical turns into an Executive-style negotiator. Typically the Analytical buyer was trained as an engineer or an accountant, so everything's been okay as long as it's been buttoned down, nailed down, and in its place.

Analyticals don't like the push and shove of negotiating. They like everything to be rigid and in place, and their favorite expression is, "It's the principle of the thing."

The opposite personality style, the Extrovert/Den Mother will say, "Hey, look! We're only talking five hundred bucks here, so for heaven's sake let's split the difference and get this thing going."

And the Analytical/Executive-style negotiator will say, "Well I understand we're talking $500. Actually, since you're proposing that we split it, we're only talking $250, aren't we? But at this point, it's the principle of the thing I'm concerned about."

So, if you're an Analytical, be careful that you're not too rigid in the way you negotiate.

Understanding personality styles and how to deal with them is one of the most important skills an investor can acquire. There are many books, audio programs, and video programs available that will help you learn about personality differences, and we would strongly urge you to spend a few dollars and several hours studying the subject. When you're trying to buy someone's home as an investment property, right off the bat you're thinking differently about the property from the way that person is thinking about it.

Key Points to Remember from This Chapter

- Personality styles develop early in life, and if your style doesn't match the sellers', you will have difficulties relating to those sellers.
- People are either assertive or nonassertive and either emotional or unemotional.
- The assertive-unemotional Pragmatic is a down-to-earth, time-management-conscious businessperson.
- The emotional-assertive Extrovert is a fun-loving, fast decision maker.
- The emotional-nonassertive Amiable is a warm, fuzzy people person.
- The unemotional-nonassertive Analytical has a buttoned-down accountant mentality.
- Less assertive people are slow decision makers and may genuinely need time to think things over.
- We all love people with our own personality style. We have the most problems with people that have the personality style in the opposite corner of the chart.
- Different personality styles develop into different negotiating styles.

14

The Art of Win-Win Negotiating

You have probably heard that the objective of a negotiation is to create a win-win solution, something creative that allows both you and the sellers to walk away from the negotiating table feeling that you've won. You may have had this demonstrated to you by the example of the two people who have only one orange, but both want it. They talk about it for a while, and they decide that the best they can do is to split the orange down the middle, with each settling for half of it. To be sure that it's fair, they decide that one of them will cut the orange and the other will choose which half she wants. However, as they discuss their underlying needs in the negotiation, they learn that one of them wants the orange to make juice and the other wants to use its rind in baking a cake. They have magically found a way that both of them can win and neither has to lose.

Oh, sure! Once in a while you'll find a situation in which both sides are so uninformed that the magic third solution fails to occur to either of them. We always marvel at the story of the two people with the orange. They had gone to the trouble of deciding who would cut and who would choose, but they hadn't even asked each other what they wanted the orange for! That's remarkably uninformed.

The same thing could happen when you're buying real estate, but it doesn't happen often enough to make the concept meaningful. Let's face it, when you're sitting down with a seller to buy his or her property, the chances are that the seller wants the highest price and you want the lowest price. There's not going to be a magical win-win solution. Sellers want to take money out of your pocket and put it into theirs.

Instead of trying to dominate sellers and trick them into doing things that they wouldn't normally do, we believe that you should work with the other person to seek out problems and develop solutions where both of you can win.

Your reaction to that may be, "Fellas, that's pretty Pollyanna, don't you think? There's no such thing as win-win in real estate investing. When I'm buying, I'm obviously trying to get the lowest price I possibly can, and the buyer is obviously trying to get the highest possible price. How on earth can we both win?"

Let's start out with the most important issue: what do we mean when we say win-win? Does it really mean that both sides win? Or does it mean that both sides lose equally so that the outcome is fair? What if each side thinks that it won and the other side lost—would that be win-win?

Before you dismiss that last possibility, think about it some more. Suppose you're buying a property and you leave the negotiation thinking, "I won. I would have paid more if the seller had been a better negotiator." However, the seller is thinking that she won because she would have taken less if you had been a better negotiator. Both of you think that you won and the other person lost. Is that win-win? Yes, we believe it is, as long as it's a permanent feeling— as long as neither of you wakes up tomorrow morning thinking,

"Son of a gun, now I know what that person did to me. Wait until I see him again."

That's why we stress doing things that feed the perception that the other side won, such as:

- Don't jump at the first offer.
- Ask for more than you expect to get.
- Flinch at the other side's proposals.
- Avoid confrontation.
- Play Reluctant Buyer.
- Use the Vise gambit: you'll have to do better than that.
- Use Higher Authority to avoid confrontation.
- Never offer to split the difference.
- Set aside impasse issues.
- Always ask for a trade-off and never make a concession without a reciprocal concession.
- Taper down your concessions.
- Position the other side for Easy Acceptance.

Besides constantly feeding the perception that the other side won, observe these four fundamental rules.

Rule 1 of Win-Win Negotiating: Don't Narrow Things Down to Just One Issue

If, for example, you have resolved all the other issues and the only thing that is left to negotiate is price, somebody does have to win and somebody does have to lose. As long as you keep more than one issue on the table, you can always work trade-offs so that the other person doesn't mind conceding on price because you are able to offer something in return.

Sometimes sellers try to narrow the transaction by saying, "We're only interested in getting the best price, and we want to cash out. We're not interested in carrying back financing, and we don't care what you do with the property once you've bought it." They are trying to treat this as a one-issue negotiation in order to persuade you that the only way you can make a concession that is meaningful to them is to raise your price. When this happens, you should do everything possible to put other issues, such as terms, closing date, and financial credentials, onto the table so that you can use these items as trade-offs and get away from the perception that this is a one-issue negotiation.

At a seminar, a commercial real estate salesperson came up to us. He was excited because he'd almost completed negotiating a contract for a very large commercial building. "We've been working on it for over a year now," he said. "And we've almost got it resolved. In fact, we've resolved everything except price, and we're only $72,000 apart." We flinched when we heard that because we knew that now that he'd narrowed the negotiations down to one issue, there had to be a winner and there had to be a loser. However close the two sides might be, they were probably heading for trouble.

If you find yourself deadlocked in a one-issue negotiation, you should try adding other issues into the mix. Fortunately, there are many more elements that are important in negotiations than just the one main issue. The art of win-win negotiating is to piece together those elements like putting together a jigsaw puzzle so that both the buyer and the seller can win.

Rule 1 is, don't narrow the negotiations down to just one issue. You can resolve impasses by finding common ground on small issues, so to keep the negotiation moving, you should always keep several issues open until the main one is resolved.

Rule 2 of Win-Win Negotiating: People Are Not All Out for the Same Thing

The second rule that makes you a win-win negotiator is understanding that people are not all out for the same thing. We all have an overriding tendency to assume that other people want the same things that we want, and because of this we believe that what's important to us will be important to them. But that's not necessarily true.

The biggest trap that neophyte negotiators fall into is assuming that price is the dominant issue in a negotiation. There are many elements other than price that may also be important to the other person.

- Payment terms are a big issue, of course. In our minds, the terms are much more important than the price. We would say to any seller, "We'll let you dictate the price if you'll let us dictate the terms." We'll give you twice what you are asking for your property if you'll let us pay you $10 a month with no interest added.
- The seller needs to know that you can perform. Many of our best deals have come from sellers who had previously accepted a higher offer, but the buyer hadn't been able to get the financing or in some other way failed to perform.
- Some sellers really care what happens to the property after they leave.

These things all come into play, along with half a dozen other factors. When you have satisfied the seller that you can meet all of his or her other requirements, then, and only then, does price become a deciding factor.

Don't assume that the sellers want what you want, because if you do, it leaves you with the assumption that anything you do in the negotiations to help them get what they want will hurt you.

Win-win negotiating can come about only when you understand that people don't all want the same things from the negotiation. Negotiating is not just a matter of getting what you want; it's also a matter of being concerned about the other person's getting what he or she wants. One of the most powerful thoughts that you can have when you're negotiating with someone is, "What can I give them that won't take away from my position?" rather than, "What can I get from them?" When you give people what they want in a negotiation, they become much more likely to give you what you want.

Rule 3 of Win-Win Negotiating: Don't Try to Squeeze the Last Dollar out of a Transaction

The third key to win-win negotiating is this: don't be too greedy. Don't try to get the last dollar off the table. You may feel that you triumphed, but does it help you if you leave the seller feeling defeated? That last dollar on the table can be a very expensive one to pick up. A man who attended Roger's seminar in Tucson told him that he was able to buy the company that he owned because another potential buyer had made that mistake. The other person had negotiated hard and pushed the seller to the brink of frustration. An old pickup truck was included in the sale of the company, and as a final Nibble, the other buyer said, "You are going to put new tires on that pickup truck before you transfer title, aren't you?" That was the straw that broke the proverbial camel's back. The owner reacted angrily, refused to sell his company to this other buyer, and instead sold it to the man attending Roger's seminar.

Don't try to get it all. Leave something so that the seller can feel that he won also.

Rule 4 of Win-Win Negotiating: Put Something Back on the Table

The fourth key to win-win negotiating is this: put something back on the table when the negotiation is over. We don't mean telling the sellers that you'll give them a higher price than they negotiated. We mean doing something more than you promised to do. Give them a little appreciation for the good condition in which they left the property. Care about their feelings a little more than you have to. You'll find that the little extras for which they didn't have to negotiate mean more to them than all the things for which they did.

The Art of Win-Win Negotiating

Real estate negotiations offer great win-win opportunities because there is so much more to negotiate than just price. As long-term investors, we stress value rather than price. Value is the combination of what you pay and how you pay it. Let's look at an example of this concept. What is a house worth that produces a net operating income (NOI) of $1,000 per month? To illustrate our point, let's assume that we were able to get 100 percent financing on the property, which is doubtful, but it does occasionally happen.

If we have $1,000 per month with which to buy the house, we could borrow approximately $100,000 for 15 years at 9 percent interest and make the payments with the NOI. On the other hand, if we found a seller who was willing to finance the property at 0 percent interest for 30 years, we could pay $360,000 for the house and still make the payments with the NOI. Granted, these are two extremes, but look at the possibilities. How many combinations of price and terms lie between $100,000 paid over 15 years at 9 percent interest and $360,000 paid over 30 years at 0 percent interest? Between these extremes, there are dozens of combinations that will work for different sellers depending on their individual needs.

It is this wide range of possibilities that gives us so much ability to create win-win situations when negotiating real estate deals. Furthermore, in addition to negotiating price and terms, there are dozens of other things that can also be negotiated—things like personal property to be included in the deal, who pays loan discount points, inspection fees, surveys, the size of the down payment, and many more.

Because different people have different needs, it is possible that a seller who is in financial distress may be willing to sell the property described above for $75,000 cash if you can close in five days, while someone who has no mortgage and is getting ready to retire may be attracted to the idea of financing the property at 0 percent or a very low interest rate in order to convert their equity into a retirement income. Remember that information is power in a negotiation, so you should find out as much as possible about the seller's needs before you make an offer. We have been successfully negotiating win-win real estate deals for more than 35 years, so we know that the concept works, and that it works especially well with real estate transactions.

Now let us recap what we've taught you about win-win negotiating.

Key Points to Remember from This Chapter

- Winning is a perception, and by constantly feeding that perception, you can often convince sellers that they have won without having to make any substantial concessions to them.
- Don't narrow the negotiations down to just one issue.
- Don't assume that helping the sellers get what they want takes away from your position. You're not out for the same thing.
- Don't be greedy. Don't try to get the last dollar off the table.
- Put something back on the table. Do more than the sellers bargained for.
- Learn as much as possible about the sellers. The more you know about them, the easier it will be to structure win-win negotiations with them.

15

Negotiating Offers That Meet the Seller's Needs

In the previous chapter, we discussed win-win negotiating and how this can best be achieved by understanding that your needs and those of the seller are not the same. In fact, sellers' needs vary widely. While selling for cash may be great for one seller, it may cause major problems for another. Once you understand that each seller is different and has different needs and that each property is different and has its own unique elements, you will be better able to comprehend that there are potentially as many different ways to buy property as there are combinations of properties and people.

Naturally sellers want to get as much as possible from selling their property, but when you are valuing investment real estate, price is only part of the equation. The ability to balance price and terms allows you to offer a wide range of prices and methods of payment when you are negotiating purchases. We thought we had explained this well in our book *The Weekend Millionaire's Secrets to Investing in Real Estate,* but since that book's release in the fall of 2003, we've fielded thousands of questions asking for more information on how the concept works.

The needs of sellers who have very little equity in their property, are behind on their mortgage payments, and are facing imminent foreclosure are completely different from those of sellers who own their property free and clear and would like to convert it into an income stream for retirement. The needs of sellers who are embroiled in a heated divorce are completely different from those of sellers whose last child has just left the nest and who no longer need such a big house. The needs of a seller who has just been transferred to a new job hundreds of miles away are completely different from those of a seller who owns a multistory home and has recently been in an accident that has left him confined to a wheelchair. The list of individual scenarios like these could fill a book by itself, but the point is, the needs of each seller are different, and the better the job you are able to do in finding and filling each seller's unique needs, the more successful you will become as an investor.

If your only negotiating strategy is to make conventional offers that require a 20 percent down payment and bank financing for the balance, you'll run across an occasional seller who is desperate enough to accept your wholesale offer, but with most sellers, 95 percent of your negotiations will center on price. If you use only this one negotiating strategy, your success will be sporadic and you'll miss out on untold opportunities because your offers will offend or insult most sellers. Conversely, if you take the time and make the effort to learn about a seller's needs and incorporate solutions to them into your offers, you will find your success rate improving dramatically.

Shortly after the release of our real estate book, we began hosting live online chats on our Web site as a service to our readers. This gives them the opportunity to ask us and our guest experts questions about real estate investing, wealth building, and negotiating. Since then, thousands of people have taken advantage of these *free* live online chats, which are usually held on Monday evenings at 8:00 p.m. Eastern, 7:00 p.m. Central, 6:00 p.m. Mountain, and 5:00 p.m. Pacific times. If you would like to receive e-mail reminders of the dates and times of these chats, all you need to do is visit our Web site at *www.weekendmillionaire.com* and register as a "New User." The chats are free, and everyone is welcome to participate. If you haven't taken part in one of these chats, we strongly urge you to do so. We've had chats in which people from as far away as England, Germany, South Africa, Indonesia, China, New Zealand, Australia, and Hungary were participating.

Must-Have Tools for Long-Term Investors

From the questions we keep receiving in our chats, we've discovered that many people are struggling with the concept of how to balance price and terms to create different offers that would all provide positive cash flow given the NOI. As a result, we did two things.

First, we produced a companion to the real estate book titled *Weekend Millionaire Real Estate FAQ*. In this book, we sorted the questions we got during the chats and via e-mails into chapters with the same headings as those in the real estate book. Thus, anyone who has a question while reading the real estate book can go to the corresponding chapter in the FAQ book, where he or she is likely to find the question and a more detailed answer than we were able to give in the fast-moving chats.

Second, we worked for months with a very skilled computer programmer who just happens to be one of our successful "Weekend Millionaire" students to produce the "Weekend Millionaire Offer Generator" computer program. This is the ultimate negotiating tool for long-term real estate investors. It takes the guesswork out of making offers. Let's look at some of the things the program will do.

Computing Net Operating Income

The first thing an investor needs to do after inspecting a property is to determine how much money will be available with which to purchase the property. This is the amount left over after deducting the costs of vacancies, management, maintenance, utilities, taxes, insurance, and other expenses from the estimated rents. This amount, called net operating income (NOI), is the actual amount of return that you will receive on your investment if you pay cash for the property or, if you finance the purchase, the amount that you can use to make the payments without having to use other income to subsidize them.

The "Weekend Millionaire Offer Generator," which works equally well on PC, Macintosh, or UNIX-based computers, does this calculating for you. The program prompts you to answer a few initial questions about yourself and then saves the data to use with any future offers you create. Once you have the data saved, you can skip the initial steps and get right to the screens where you input estimated rents and expenses. The program will then compute the NOI and show you exactly how much money you have with which to structure an offer.

Generating All-Cash Offers

Once you know the NOI, you might think that generating all-cash offers would be as simple as deciding what return you want to receive on your cash and doing the math. It is, except that most people forget about closing costs and repairs, which also require cash and can substantially reduce the anticipated return if you don't consider them.

The "Weekend Millionaire Offer Generator" keeps you from making this mistake. When you click on the "Generate a Cash Offer" button, a screen appears that asks you for an estimate of closing costs and repairs and the percentage return you want on the cash these items will require. It then reduces the computed NOI by the amount needed to provide you with your desired return on the closing costs and repairs and shows you the amount that is left for you to use in determining your cash offer. You then enter the rate of return you want to receive on the purchase, and the program will compute the amount that you can pay for the property and still get the desired return. As you adjust the rate up and down, you can watch the price change. For example, if the NOI remaining after taking the return on closing costs and repairs into account is $1,000 per month and you plan to pay cash for the property, you can get a 10 percent return on your money if you pay $120,000 for the property. If you are comfortable with an 8 percent return, you could pay $150,000, but if you're greedy and want a 20 percent return, you'd have to buy the property for just $60,000. You don't need to know any mathematical formulas or use a calculator; the program does it all for you. You only need to enter the rate of return you want to receive.

Generating Financed Offers

Since few investors pay cash for real estate because they would lose the benefits of leverage if they did, most people choose to click on the "Generate a Financed Offer" button. Many new investors get in trouble with financed offers. They call their bank and ask how much the payments will be on a given amount of money, and then they try to decide if they can rent the prospective property for enough to make the payments. Not only do they overlook closing costs and repairs, but many times they fail to think about the other expenses that have to be taken into account when computing NOI.

By prompting users to enter estimated rents and expenses first and then computing the NOI, the "Weekend Millionaire Offer Generator" eliminates many of the mistakes that new investors make, but it also does much more. As with cash offers, it prompts you to enter estimated closing costs and repairs, but for financed offers it goes a step further; it also asks for the amount of the down payment that you will make and the rate of return you want on all of these cash outlays. It deducts enough from the NOI to cover the desired return on these seldom-considered cash items and then gives you a world of options on ways to use the remaining NOI to purchase the property.

This is where the "Weekend Millionaire Offer Generator" becomes the most powerful negotiating tool on the market today. With it, users have the option of creating offers that utilize bank financing, seller financing, private third-party financing, or any combination of the three. It gives them the option of raising or lowering the amount of their down payment, and combining market-rate financing from commercial lenders with very low or zero percent financing from sellers to achieve acceptable blended rates. Small first mortgages from banks can be combined with larger second mortgages from sellers to create no-money-down offers that will provide positive cash flow if the seller accepts the offer. The options are virtually endless.

When you know the seller's needs, this program will quickly allow you to determine whether or not it is possible to create a reasonable offer that he or she might accept. In addition, throughout the process of creating "what-if" scenarios under which you might buy a property, the "Weekend Millionaire Offer Generator" also pops up a warning message whenever you try to create an offer that will not provide positive cash flow. This feature alone has saved users hundreds of thousands of dollars and kept many of them from getting stuck with what we call "alligator properties," meaning properties that eat up your cash like an alligator.

Printing Letters of Intent

Each time you juggle price and terms to create a new offer, the "Weekend Millionaire Offer Generator" lets you save the offer as part of a collection of possibilities for that particular property. Once you have generated an array of possible offers, you move to the next step, which is inputting the name and address of the sellers. The program combines your personal information with that of the sellers to generate a "Letter of Intent" for any or all of the offers that you want to present. While this feature is very generic and addresses only the specifics of the financial part of your offers, you are given the opportunity to edit the letters to include any conditions or other comments that you wish to add before printing them. If you don't like the layout of the letters produced by the program, you can save them in several different formats that can be brought up in any word-processing program, enabling you to reformat them so that they look the way you want.

The default setting in the program inserts $1,000 into each letter of intent as the proposed earnest money deposit, but you can change this to any amount you desire simply by typing over the default setting. There is also a "Conditions" screen that allows you to insert any special conditions you may want to include in your offers. If you typed, "This offer is conditional upon the sellers leaving the stove and refrigerator that were in the kitchen when the house was inspected on _____date," this language will automatically be incorporated into the "Letter of Intent."

Imagine the negotiating flexibility you would have if, within minutes of inspecting a property, you could compute the NOI for that property, generate a wide range of offers, and have "Letters of Intent" ready for your signature and for presentation to sellers. Sellers would certainly feel that you were professional and that you knew what you were doing. We even have some students who carry a laptop computer and small printer in their car so that they can present sellers with an offer before they leave the property.

For those of you who wonder how difficult the "Weekend Millionaire Offer Generator" computer program is to learn, we've got some great news for you. The program is designed with a unique "help" feature that can be turned on or off any time the user wants. When the help feature is on, a line of text will appear at the top of each screen that will give a description of the screen and its purpose whenever you place the cursor on it. Also within each screen, if you don't understand what to enter in one of the fields, if you just place your cursor on the field's label, an explanation of what is to be entered will pop up. In addition, there are other pop-up help texts that describe virtually everything in the program as you are working through it. Once you are comfortable with the program, you can simply click on the "help" button on the top left of any screen to turn the pop-up help on or off. As they say, we have made every effort to make the program "idiot proof." You can learn much more about it by going to *www.weekendmillionaire.com/store*, where you will find a more detailed explanation of what it can do.

Using an Inspection as a Negotiating Tool

As we have emphasized throughout this book, information is power in a negotiation. We've discussed the different needs of sellers and how learning about them can affect the negotiations, but as we mention in the opening paragraph of this chapter, each property has its own unique features that, when combined with the seller's needs, greatly expand the possibilities. A good way to learn about a property's unique features is to conduct a detailed inspection.

We also learned from questions we've received in our online chats that most new investors are apprehensive about conducting inspections. They tend to walk through a house, giving it a cursory look, and if it looks good, they are satisfied. Most of them are afraid to ask tough questions for fear of offending the sellers, but as with learning about the seller's needs, the more information you can gather about the condition of a property, the more strength you will have when negotiating its purchase.

Over the years, we have developed a checklist that we use when doing an inspection, and we have made it available to our readers as a free download from our Web site. It is in PDF format, and it can be downloaded and saved or simply printed from the Web site as often as necessary. The form can double as both an initial inspection form and a move-in/move-out form that you can use with tenants. It provides a room-by-room checklist of items to be ranked as excellent, average, or poor. Beside each item, there is a space to note any work that needs to be done and a blank to fill in the estimated cost. When you have totaled the repair costs, you have the information you need to insert in the repair cost field in the "Weekend Millionaire Offer Generator" program.

This inspection form provides a tool for you to use when doing an inspection that takes away most of the tension involved in asking tough questions. Since it is a preprinted inspection form and you are checking off each item as you inspect it, it is only natural for you to ask questions whenever you find an unsatisfactory condition. If you aren't satisfied with the information you gather, don't hesitate to spend a few dollars and get a complete home inspection from a licensed home inspection firm. It's better to lose a $200 inspection fee than to buy a property that requires thousands of dollars worth of repairs that you didn't catch.

When sellers know that you are aware of deficiencies or defects in their property, it weakens their negotiating position and reduces the likelihood that they will make ridiculous counteroffers. It also gives you a negotiating tool that you can use if you do get an unacceptable counteroffer; if the seller wants a higher price, you can always ask him or her to pay for the needed repairs.

Conclusion

We want you to be successful. The tools described in this chapter have all been designed to assist you in achieving financial success. This nation's educational system is a miserable failure when it comes to teaching young people about entrepreneurship and wealth building. It focuses mainly on teaching students how to get a job, not on how to build a future. As a result, most people spend 40 hours a week, 50 weeks a year for 40 years and end up with little more to show for it than a monthly social security check. Building wealth with real estate is a long-term proposition, not a get-rich-quick scheme. For example, if you devoted just four hours a week to learning the Weekend Millionaire method of investing and it took you an entire year to buy your first investment property, in just 15 years that one property could pay you more than the social security check that you worked your whole life to obtain.

Key Points to Remember from This Chapter

- No two sellers and no two properties are exactly alike.
- Potentially, there are as many different ways to buy properties as there are combinations of properties and people.
- Free live help is available to investors who participate in the chats on our Web site at *www.weekendmillionaire.com*.
- *Weekend Millionaire Real Estate FAQ* is a companion book to *The Weekend Millionaire's Secrets to Investing in Real Estate.* It is a compilation of questions and answers from our students that is laid out with the same chapter headings for easy reference.
- The "Weekend Millionaire Offer Generator" is the finest tool on the market today for long-term real estate investors. It is a modestly priced computer program that allows you to balance price and terms to meet the needs of sellers with differing requirements.
- The inspection form that is available as a free download on the *www.weekendmillionaire.com* Web site is an excellent tool for both investors and property managers to use during initial inspections or as a move-in/move-out inspection form.

16

Twenty Closing Tactics

If you are (or have been) a salesperson, you will be very familiar with closing tactics. If you aren't (and haven't been), then this chapter will be new to you. Closing tactics are techniques that salespeople use to get a buyer to make a decision faster than he or she otherwise would.

That's an advantage, because the faster you can get the seller to decide, the better the chance you have of getting what you want. The longer you give someone to think about the decision, the less chance you have of getting what you want. Here are 20 closes that you can use to get a faster decision from the seller.

The Tugboat Close

If you've ever stood on a levee at New Orleans, you've no doubt marveled at the tugboats that haul the barges down the Mississippi River. A tiny tugboat no more than 30 feet long can pull a string of barges, each one carrying more than 10,000 tons of cargo. When Roger sails his sailboat near Los Angeles harbor, he watches with amazement as a tiny tugboat maneuvers a 300,000-ton super-tanker. What's the secret of the tugboat's incredible power? The tugboat skipper knows that he can move the largest load if he does it *a little bit at a time*. If the skipper tried to force that supertanker to change its direction, he couldn't do it. No matter how hard he revved up his engines and attacked that supertanker, he would only bounce off. But by doing it a little bit at a time, he can accomplish the most incredible things.

What does this have to do with getting the seller to say yes? By doing it a little bit at a time, you can accomplish the most amazing things. By doing it a little bit at a time, you can move the most intractable seller around and get him or her to sell to you.

Roger once got a $250,000 loan from a banker using the Tugboat Close. He owned 33 houses with another investor, and he wanted to buy his partner out so that he would own them all. To do this, he needed to get the banker to make a $250,000 loan secured only by a second mortgage on the property. At first, the bank refused to make such a risky investment. Roger and the other investor asked to meet with the vice president, who only restated the same position. However, they gently persisted, knowing that as long as the banker didn't throw them out, they were getting closer to getting the loan approved. An hour later, the banker had agreed to make the loan if Roger would cross-secure it with a $100,000 certificate of deposit. They continued to restate their position without any confrontation, knowing that they were nudging him around. Another hour later, he agreed to make the loan secured only by the property.

The next time you're in a situation where you're convinced that the seller will never change his or her mind, think of those tugboats nudging that huge oil tanker around. Sellers do change their minds. Just because they said no to carrying back financing a minute ago, an hour ago, or yesterday doesn't necessarily mean that they'll say no again if you ask them one more time. A little bit at a time, you can change anyone's mind, especially if you give him or her some new information that can be used in making a revised decision.

The Paddock Close

When Roger was a teenager, he earned extra money by photographing Thoroughbred horses for breeders. This is an unusual branch of photography because the breeders don't want any artistic styling to the picture. They need a photograph that looks like every other photograph of a horse standing at stud, so that the breeders can accurately evaluate the horse. It's a side shot with the horse's far legs slightly advanced so that the breeders can see all four legs.

It's difficult to get temperamental Thoroughbred stallions to stand that way. If you lead the horse in front of the camera and he's not standing properly, you can tug on his leg all you want, but he'll just put it back the way he decided to stand in the first place. That's the way some investors try to change the seller's mind—with brute force.

The only way to change the way the stallion is standing is to get his mind off the way he decided to stand before. Roger would lead him around the paddock, talking gently to him, to get his mind off the decision he had made earlier. Then he would lead the stallion back in front of the camera and see how he was standing now. If he was still standing the wrong way, Roger would patiently lead him around the paddock once more and try again.

Some sellers are like those stallions. They say no to you for no reason other than the one that makes a horse decide to stand with its legs together. When that happens, remember the stallion and take the sellers for a mental walk around the paddock. Don't try to force them to change their minds. Instead, tell a little story to take their minds off the decision that they made. Think to yourself, "I may have asked the right closing question, but my timing was off. I'll distract them and return to the closing question in a few minutes." After you've mentally engaged them in other thoughts, go for the close again. If they still say no, do it again, like Roger walking the stallion around the paddock again. After you've distracted them with a story, go for the close again.

Never think of a no as a refusal; simply think of it as a sign that you need to walk the sellers around the paddock again, giving them additional information and more reasons to say yes.

The "That Wouldn't Stop You" Close

This is the simplest close that we're going to teach you, and it will probably seem ludicrous to you. Until you've tried it, you won't believe how powerful it can be.

Roger's son Dwight taught us this close when he was selling new cars. Whenever one of his customers raised an objection, instead of trying to argue that the customer was wrong or find a way to work around the objection, he learned to say, "But that wouldn't stop you from going ahead today, would it?" At first, he felt stupid saying this because he was sure that the customer would ridicule him. However, he discovered that a remarkable number of times, the buyers would back away from the objection. They would say, "You only have the car in red? We wanted green."

He would respond, "But that wouldn't stop you from going ahead today, would it?"

And they would say, "Well, no, I guess it wouldn't."

It sounds outrageous, doesn't it? But if you try it, we think you will end up kicking yourself, because you'll find that objections that have been giving you fits for years really don't need a response. The seller says, "I've already turned down an offer higher than that."

You say, "But that wouldn't stop you from selling to us, would it?"

He may well say, "Well, I guess not, if you can close in 30 days."

You don't have to satisfy every objection. If you decide to do that, you'll begin to feel that you're playing one of those "hit the gopher" games in an arcade. Every time you hit one gopher on the head and knock him back into the hole, another one pops up in another location. Before you know it, you're worn out, and there are still gophers sticking up their heads. Don't allow yourself to get into the objection-answering business. Many sellers use objections as delaying tactics to avoid having to make a decision.

The Leave 'Em Alone Close

If you are buying from a husband and wife (or from two partners, for that matter), it's important for you to give them time to consult each other on whether or not to accept the offer. If you stay with them the whole time, you may stop them from making a decision. However well they know each other, they can't read each other's minds. They aren't sure if their spouse wants to accept the offer or not. Leaving them alone for a while gives them a chance to ask, "What do you think, dear?"

This doesn't just apply to husbands and wives. You might be making an offer to the president and vice president of a company. The president may be eager to go ahead, but she wants to be sure that the vice president is "on board" and will enthusiastically support the decision. Or the vice president may be eager, but he isn't sure that the president won't overrule him. Giving the two of them some time alone to resolve those issues will make getting a favorable decision easier for you.

Don't make them ask you for time to talk it over, give it to them. You don't have to say, "Let me give you time to think about it." Simply find an excuse to leave them alone for a few minutes, such as asking if they mind your walking around and taking another look at the property while they are considering your offer. Not only will this give them time alone, but it may also bring them to a quicker decision because they won't want you to find anything that might lead you to have second thoughts about making the purchase.

The Vince Lombardi Close

When you're trying to get your offer accepted, a psychological resistance sometimes builds up in the sellers' mind. As they approach the point of making a decision, they start to resist. Perhaps they are concerned that they may be doing the wrong thing or that they're not getting the best deal. Whatever the reason, the tension builds until the moment that they make the decision. Then, once the sellers have made the decision to trust you and are ready to go ahead with your proposal, a remarkable change takes place in their minds. Having made the decision to trust you, their minds will do anything they can to reinforce the decision that they just made. That's when you can often get them to agree to things that they wouldn't agree to earlier, such as a smaller earnest money deposit or carrying back part or all of the financing.

Vince Lombardi always used to talk about the second effort, didn't he? He loved to show his Green Bay Packers film clips of receivers who almost caught the ball, but couldn't quite hang on to it. But instead of letting it go, they made a second effort and caught it before it hit the ground. Or running backs who should have been tackled, but who still managed to wriggle free and make the touchdown. Vince Lombardi would tell his players that everybody out there is making the first effort. They wouldn't be on the team if they didn't know how to play the game well and weren't out there doing everything that he told them to do. But that's what every player on every team in the league is doing. The difference, Vince Lombardi would say, between the good players and the great players is that the great players will make that second effort. When everyone else thinks that the play is lost, they'll still keep trying.

If you want to be a great investor, take a tip from Vince Lombardi. When everyone else is saying, "Give it up. You've tried hard enough," don't be reluctant to give it one more effort. Don't walk away from a deal without at least giving the sellers a second or third opportunity to say yes.

The Silent Close

The Silent Close is always a fun close to use. It says that you should present your offer and then *shut up*! From then on, the person who talks first loses.

Sellers can respond to your offer in one of three ways: they can say yes, they can say no, or they can ask you for more information to help them decide. If you're a positive thinker, you will expect them to say yes. You will be surprised if they say no or indicate that they can't decide. Wait to find out. Don't change your proposal until you know for sure that they won't say yes.

Roger once made an offer on a rental to a seller who was asking $240,000. His offer was $180,000. Frankly, presenting such a low offer scared him. He thought the seller would be furious at having wasted his time on such a low offer. Roger gritted his teeth and read the offer to him. Then he turned the offer around, pushed it across the table, and laid his pen on top of it for the seller to sign.

The seller looked at it for a while, then he picked it up and read it all way through, including the fine print. He put it down and looked at Roger, who had to bite his tongue to stop himself from talking.

He picked the offer up again and again read it all the way through. Then he put it down and looked at Roger for what seemed like five minutes.

Finally he said, "I suppose that now I'm supposed to say yes, no, or maybe. Is that right?"

Roger smiled slightly but still didn't say anything. The seller picked it up for the third time and read it all the way through once again. Then he said, "I'll tell you what I'll do. I won't accept this, but I will accept this." He wrote a very acceptable counterproposal on the bottom of the offer, turned it around, and slid it back across the desk to Roger.

The Silent Close is the simplest close to understand and one of the hardest to use. We're not used to silence. Even a minute of silence seems like an eternity.

Remember, always assume that the seller will say yes. Present the offer, and then don't say a word until you find out what the seller will do.

The Subject-To Close

The Subject-To Close is a great way to handle a buyer who is intimidated by the size of the decision that you're asking him or her to make. Real estate agents know that when their customers are buying a new home, it is probably the largest purchase that they will ever make. The agent knows that he has found the perfect home for them, but sometimes the sheer size of the decision stops them from going ahead. Agents then say, "Why don't we just write it up subject to you being approved for the financing?" By making the sale conditional on another event taking place, you appear to be turning a major decision into a minor one. Naturally, a good real estate agent knows that the buyers will qualify for the financing, so they really have bought the home.

A life insurance agent realizes that her buyer is having trouble agreeing to her proposal. She says, "Frankly, I don't know if I can get someone of your age insured for this much. It would be subject to your passing the physical, so why don't we just write up the paperwork subject to your passing the physical." It doesn't sound as though the buyer has made as big a decision as he or she really has. However, the agent knows that if her customer can fog a mirror during that physical, she can find someone, somewhere, who will underwrite that policy. The customer really has bought it.

As an investor, you might say to the sellers, "Why don't we make this subject to my being able to get acceptable financing approved within two weeks?" Obviously, you wouldn't put this concession into a contract unless you knew that you could get the financing. Although the concession doesn't mean much to you, it may be just enough to ease the pressure on the sellers by giving them a couple of weeks to become comfortable with their decision.

When you contact them to let them know that your loan has been approved, their decision to sell their property has become acceptable and they are more ready to move forward with the closing.

The Contingency Close

You use the Subject-To close when you know that there will be a way for you to overcome the contingency. But what if you don't know that you and the seller will get past the contingency successfully?

What if the only way you can get the seller to accept your offer is subject to his being able to buy a condo on the beach in Hawaii for under $200,000? Can this close still be effective even if the contingency is one that you can never overcome?

Yes, and it's probably still the smart thing to do, even if the contingency seems insurmountable, because you're psychologically drawing the seller closer to making the decision. When his mind is drooling at the thought of retiring to that beach in Hawaii, it's easier to get him to remove the contingency after the fact than it is to get him to agree to your initial offer without it. Just be sure that you're not using a contingency as a closing crutch. You should put a contingency into an offer only as a last resort.

The Ben Franklin Close

Every salesperson is familiar with the Ben Franklin Close. It's based on something Franklin wrote to British chemist Joseph Priestley about the way that he made decisions. He wrote:

> *My way [of making decisions] is to divide a sheet of paper into two columns; writing over the one Pro, and over the other Con. Then, during the three or four days' considera-tion, I put down under the different heads short hints of the different motives, that at different times occur to me, for or against the measure. When I have thus got them all together in one view, I endeavor to estimate their respective weights;*

and where I find two, on each side, that seem equal, I strike them both out. If I find a reason pro equal to some two reasons con, I strike out all three. If I judge some two reasons con, equal to some three reasons pro, I strike out the five; and thus proceeding I find at length where the balance lies; and if, after a day or two of further considerations, nothing new that is of importance occurs on either side, I come to a determination accordingly.

The Ben Franklin close is designed to make people feel better when they have trouble making up their minds. When you are using this as a closing technique, there is an essential preamble. Unless you use this preamble, the Ben Franklin close won't work. Before you use the close, you say, "Mr. Seller, I'm not surprised that you're having trouble making a decision, because many intelligent people do. For example, one of our greatest statesmen, Ben Franklin, had trouble making decisions. Let me tell you what he used to do. See if you think it's a good way for you to make up your mind. When Ben couldn't make up his mind, he would simply take a sheet of paper and draw a line down the middle. On the left-hand side, he'd list all the reasons for going ahead with the project, and on the right-hand side, he'd list all the reasons for not doing so. If the reasons for going ahead exceeded the reasons for not going ahead, he would decide to proceed. Doesn't that make sense for you too, Mr. Seller?" It's important to get the seller to agree to go along with this method before you go ahead with the analysis. If you don't get his agreement first, you can go through the entire exercise and still have him tell you that he wants to think it over.

Having gotten his agreement that this is a good way to decide, start listing the reasons for his going ahead with the sale. On this side of the list, give him all the help you can. "You will have money coming in instead of going out. You won't have to worry about paying property taxes any more. You won't have to pay insurance premiums on the property any more. You won't have to keep up with the maintenance. You won't have to worry about vandalism or other possible perils." Help him make the column in favor of selling as long as possible. However, when you have exhausted the reasons for going ahead and you start on the reasons for not selling, he's on his own. When you do it like this, the list of positives will usually exceed the list of negatives, and you'll get the seller to agree to sell.

The Dumb Mistake Close

Sometimes you'd like to climb over the kitchen table and tell the seller what a dumb mistake he or she is making by not accepting your offer. You can't do this, of course, because it would just antagonize the seller. The Dumb Mistake Close is a way of telling the seller that he or she is making a dumb mistake without actually accusing him or her of it. The difference is that you tell a story about someone else who made a dumb mistake when he or she was in the same situation.

Several years ago, Mike made an offer to one of the largest banks in the country for a condominium that it had in inventory as the result of a foreclosure. His offer was for about 65 percent of what other condos in the area had been selling for. The bank officer flatly rejected the offer, saying that it was well below the amount the bank had in the property. Mike explained that he had based his offer on the amount of rent he felt he could get for the property. Still taking an adamant position, the banker said that he would take the property to auction before he'd sell it for what Mike had offered.

Nearly six months later, Mike received a call from an auction company advising him that the condo was going to be sold at auction the next week. Mike attended the auction and bought the property for $6,000 less than he had offered the bank six months earlier. Mike has used this story many times to point out that anyone, even big banks, can make dumb decisions. He uses this story with sellers who are holding out for more money as a way to address how having a bird in the hand can be worth more than having two in the bush. He will gently point out that although his offer may be less than they were expecting, it is a sure thing, and there's no guarantee that someone else will pay more.

Roger remembers a local bike store using the Dumb Mistake Close on him when he was buying a bicycle for his young son John. This was before helmets became mandatory for cyclists in California. After he and his son had picked out the bike, the storeowner selected an expensive helmet and said, "You'll need this, too." Of course, John's safety was a concern of his, but Roger had ridden a bike without a helmet throughout his childhood, so the helmet seemed like an unnecessary expense. The storeowner said, "Oh I wish Mr. Jones were here now. He lives up on Skyline Drive, and last month he bought a bike for his son Bobby. He didn't want to invest in a helmet either. The next day Bobby was riding down Church Hill Drive and went straight into a car coming up the hill. He was seriously injured, and for the rest of my life, I'll have to live with the knowledge that I didn't insist on his getting a helmet. I wish Mr. Jones were here now, because he'd tell you how important it is." Guess who grabbed that helmet out of the owner's hands and rammed it onto his son's head? You've got it! The Dumb Mistake Close is a terrific way to pressure the buyer without confrontation.

The Final Objection Close

Try the experiment that we talked about in Chapter 9. Ask someone to stand in front of you with his or her palms extended to you at shoulder height. Put your palms against that person's and start to push against them. Invariably the other person will push back. People are like that—if you push them too hard, they'll nearly always push back. The Final Objection Close removes the pressure of closing the sale and stops the seller from pushing against you.

To make this close work, you have to appear defeated, as though you've given up trying to buy from this person. "Okay," you say, "I accept that you're not going to sell to me, but just to clarify my thinking, would you mind telling me why you decided not to go ahead? What did I do wrong?"

"You didn't do anything wrong," the seller will tell you.

"Then it must be the way the offer is structured."

"No, that's not it either. It's just that we think we can get more from someone else."

"Well, that makes me feel better," you say. "I have to be able to break even on renting the property, so I can't do much better on the price. Anyway, I'm glad it wasn't anything I did wrong. So the only reason you're not going ahead is the price?"

Once you've narrowed the problems down to the Final Objection by removing the appearance of still trying to close, you have only to answer that objection to make the sale. For this close to work, you must go through these four stages:

1. Appear defeated.
2. Release the pressure.
3. Get the seller to narrow the problems down to one objection.
4. Overcome that objection.

How do you overcome the objection that your price is too low? Remember that in real estate, the value of a property is determined by the combination of the price you pay and the terms on which you pay it. Remember, you can let the seller dictate the price if he or she will let you dictate the terms. Tell the seller, "I would be able to come up to your price if you would be willing to structure the terms differently. Could we take a look at that possibility?" Often partial seller financing at a rate comparable to what banks would pay on deposits can be enough to allow you to meet the seller's price. Keep in mind that if you have to borrow the money from a bank, the interest that it charges you is going to be 3 to 5 percent more than the interest the bank pays its depositors. When sellers understand this, some of them are willing to provide partial or full financing.

The Minor Point Close

When you're trying to buy property, little decisions by the seller can lead to big decisions. If you can get the seller to agree on minor points, you are clarifying his or her thinking so that when you get ready for the major decision, he or she is less likely to feel pressured.

The car salesperson asks the buyer:

- "If you did go ahead, would you want leather or vinyl upholstery?"
- "Would you want the stick shift or the automatic?"
- "Would you prefer white or red?"

The real estate salesperson asks:

- "If you chose this home, which of these bedrooms would be the nursery for your new baby?"
- "How would you arrange the furniture in the living room?"

As a real estate investor you might say:

- "If you did sell to me, when would you want to move?"
- "Are there any services that you would need to cancel, like gardening or house cleaning?"
- "Will you be driving or flying to your new home?"

If you can get sellers to decide on little things like these, it helps them build up the confidence they need to make bigger decisions, like accepting your offer. Each time they make a small decision, it removes an item from consideration and reduces the overall size of the big decision.

The Return Serve Close

This close teaches you that when sellers seem close to making a decision and ask you a clarifying question, you should usually reply with a question. Many years ago, Roger was buying a used copy machine from an attorney. Roger asked, "Would you take $200 for it?" The attorney said, "Are you offering me $200?" Roger thought, "How smart." If he'd told Roger instead that he would take $200, Roger would probably have hemmed and hawed around before offering him even less. When buyers look as though they're close to making a decision to buy and serve you a clarifying question, return the serve; in doing so, you'll be getting a commitment. When the buyer says, "Can you close in 45 days?" say, "Would you like me to close in 45 days?" "Can I stay in the property until my kids graduate from high school?" should cause you to respond, "Would you like me to write up the contract that way?"

The Alternative Choice Close

When you ask people to choose between two alternatives, they will usually pick one of the two. Very seldom will they select the third option: that neither of the two choices is acceptable.

Whenever we use the Alternative Choice Close, its effectiveness surprises us all over again. At our seminars, we set up a table with our audio programs and books. When people are just looking, we will say, "If you did go ahead, would you use your American Express card or your MasterCard?" They nearly always pick one of the two. Then we say, "Would you like me to fill out the form for you, or would you rather do it yourself?" With just a couple of quick alternative-choice questions, we have closed the sale. The interesting thing is that even if they know what you're doing, people seem irresistibly drawn to picking one of the two alternatives.

Be sure that both of the options are acceptable to you. "Do you want it or not?" is not a smart alternative choice!

This is such a well-known close that you'll even hear little children using it. "Dad, would you like to take me to the video arcade tonight, or would tomorrow night be better for you?" As a grandson goes into the ice cream store, he says, "Grandpa, are we going to get doubles or triples today?"

Also use the Alternative Choice Close for setting appointments. Assume that the seller will want to show you the property and ask, "Would Monday or Tuesday be better for you?" "Would 10 o'clock or 11 be better for you?"

Be sure that you have narrowed the choices down to two. This close won't work with three options, so you need to eliminate the third option. A real estate salesperson who has shown the buyer three properties will say, "I got the feeling that you didn't like the layout in the first house, so if you were going to go ahead with one of the other two, which one would it be?"

Real estate salespeople also use the Alternative Choice Close to handle objections. When the buyer says, "We would never buy this house. Look at those awful green walls," a smart agent will respond with the Alternative Choice question, "If you did go ahead, would you repaint the walls yourself, or would you have a painter do it?" Whichever choice the buyer makes, the agent has won, hasn't she? The buyer can brag that he can do the job much better and cheaper than a painter can, or he can tell the agent that he has better things to do with his time. It doesn't matter what he says because either way, the agent has eliminated the objection.

As an investor, keep in mind while you are reviewing these closes that you need to buy properties at wholesale, and for this reason, you must sell the property owners and often their brokers on why they should sell to you. You must consider the underlying thought process behind each of the closes and adapt each one in such a way that it elicits the response you want.

The Doorknob Close

Like the Final Objection Close, the Doorknob Close is dependent upon your being able to release the sellers from the pressure of making the decision to sell.

When you have tried everything else and you still don't have the contract signed, you close your briefcase and say, "It was really nice talking with you, even though you decided not to go ahead. I can understand your feelings about that. Perhaps some time in the future we can get together again." You appear to be leaving, but as your hand hits the doorknob on the way out, you pause pensively and say, "Would you mind helping me? I always try to learn something whenever I fail to persuade a property owner to sell to me. Would you mind telling me what I did wrong? It will help me so much in the future."

As long as the buyers feel that you're no longer trying to convince them to sell to you, they'll often be helpful enough to share with you why they didn't go along with your offer. They may say, "You came on too strong, too early. We felt pressured." Or they may say, "You were close on the price, but if we have to carry back financing, we won't be able to afford the down payment on the condo in Hawaii."

Now you can move to the Vince Lombardi Second Effort Close. Gently thank them for sharing this information and slide back into your presentation. Remember that the Doorknob Close will work only if you're able to convince them that you're no longer trying to buy their property. You're only asking for their help on how to improve the way you present your next offer.

The Divide and Conquer Close

You may have to use the Divide and Conquer Close any time you are trying to buy from two people. We've noticed that when it comes to assertiveness levels, opposites frequently attract. A less assertive person will often marry a more assertive person. A businessperson who has a warm and easygoing personality—a people person—will often have a much more assertive business partner. They make a good team. The assertive, no-nonsense person admires the warm human qualities of the less assertive person. The easygoing people person admires the discipline and firmness of the more assertive person.

An assertive person is a fast decision maker. He or she will look at a proposal and either go for it or not go for it quickly. A less assertive person agonizes over decisions, and that analysis frequently leads to paralysis.

When you're faced with a situation like this, you should use the Divide and Conquer Close. Let's say that you're trying to buy a property from an aerospace engineer. He's analyzed your proposal 50 different ways, and you still can't get a decision. Get the more assertive wife aside and say, "Mrs. Jones, I really admire the analysis that your husband, Roy, is doing here. I wish I had that kind of detailed mind. But what concerns me, Mrs. Jones, is that you're going to lose this opportunity to move to Florida if you don't decide to go ahead now, and you really want to do that, don't you?" Then she'll go to her husband, who is still inputting the details into his computer, and say, "Roy, knock it off for heaven's sake. It's a great opportunity and we need to jump on it." Chances are that Roy will say, "Yes, dear, you handle it," and go back to his computer.

Similarly, with business partners, you may have to find a way to take the more assertive one aside and say, "I get the feeling that you're the decision maker around here, Bob. Let's move on it before it's too late." Chances are he'll say something like, "Don't worry about it. You have a deal. I just have to be diplomatic about the way I handle it with Harry."

Whenever you're dealing with two people and one of them is more assertive than the other, use the Divide and Conquer Close. Find a way to separate them, get the decision from the more assertive partner, and let him or her deal with the other partner.

The Let 'Em Think Close

With some people, it's easy to tell when they're thinking. They take a pad of paper and fill it with numbers and options, or they pull out a calculator and punch in numbers furiously. With others, it's harder to tell when they're thinking because they just go quiet and work out the decision in their mind. That's a problem for salespeople because they can't stand silence. They think it means that the customer has lost interest and that you need to stimulate him or her with conversation. Sometimes, however, you have to give people time to think.

Roger remembers when he was first investing heavily in income-producing real estate. Many times an agent would take him out to show him an apartment building that he or she wanted to sell Roger. In the car on the way back, Roger would need time to think it through. "How much would it cost me to improve the property? How high could I raise the rents? Where can I generate the cash for the down payment? How would I handle the management?" Roger prefers to work all these things out in his mind and verify his calculations later. To the agent, it must have looked as though he was totally disinterested. All too often, the agent would interpret this as meaning that he or she had to give Roger more information to stimulate his interest. Nothing could have been further from the truth. He simply needed some quiet time to think about it.

If the sellers look as if they need time to think over your proposal, give it to them. Remember, you're selling them on why they should sell to you. If they're pondering your offer and haven't yet responded to it, don't make the mistake a lot of salespeople make, which is talking too much when a decision is near. When Mike was in the advertising business, he would tell his salespeople not to spend 20 minutes making a sale and then another 40 minutes buying it back. If your offer is on the table, give the sellers adequate time to respond to it.

The Recall Close

Sometimes it isn't a good idea to tell the sellers everything you know about the transaction. It's smart to leave out something that you could suddenly recall in case you're not able to close them.

Perhaps the sellers have turned down your offer. Now it's a week later and no one else has shown any interest, and they're beginning to have seller's remorse about turning down your offer. They're sitting there thinking, "If we'd had taken that offer, we could have moved into our place in Florida by Thanksgiving."

Then you can call them up and say, "I ran across a fascinating article in *Fortune* magazine about retiring in Florida. I'd like to come by this evening and show it to you. Would seven or eight o'clock be better for you?" You've heard of buyer's remorse, of course, but seller's remorse is a reality, too. They welcome it when you call them and give them a chance to reconsider. Don't say that you have something to tell them, because then they'll ask you to tell them over the phone. And don't say that you have something you saw on the Web, because they'll ask you to e-mail it to them. It has to be something that you can show them.

An excellent reason to call a potential seller back is to present a revised offer. Since you can juggle price and terms to create hundreds of different ways to buy any given property, you can call back and say, "I've been thinking about the offer I made that you rejected earlier, and I think I might have figured out a way to buy your property that might be more acceptable. Could I stop by and show you what I've come up with?" (Here's where our computer program, the "Weekend Millionaire Offer Generator," really comes in handy. This simple-to-use program allows you to input estimated rents and expenses, computes the net operating income (NOI), walks you through the process of balancing price and terms to generate hundreds of different offers, and even lets you print the offer letters ready for your signature and presentation to sellers. The program is available on our Web site at *www.weekendmillionaire.com/store*.)

The Take Control Close

Some people have a terrible time making decisions. There are people out there who find making a decision so traumatic that they won't make a move until someone tells them it's okay. In transactional analysis terms, these people are the "child" personalities. Psychologist Eric Berne took Freud's theory of superego, id, and ego and simplified it to parent, child, and adult. The superego (or parent) restrains the other two parts of the personality. The id (or child part of the personality) tends to act impulsively, without thought. The ego (or adult part of the personality) reasons things through.

You would think that people with an impulsive, childlike personality would be the easiest sellers to persuade. After all, their philosophy is: if it feels good, do it. However, over the years, this has gotten them into trouble. Now they may really want to accept your offer, but they can't decide to do so because they're afraid they will get into trouble again. In other words, they have cold feet.

These people need to be told to buy.

You need to say to them firmly, "Everything tells me that this is the right decision for you. I'm not going to leave here today until I get your permission to go ahead. I can't leave here today in good conscience without getting your okay, so I'm going to make the decision for you. Just sign here and I'll take care of the details."

Of course, you can do this only if you're really convinced that your offer is best for them. Don't do it just to make a profit. However, if you're totally convinced that someone would be making a mistake if he or she rejected your offer, this extra push of decisiveness may be the only way you can get that person to do the right thing.

The Weekend Millionaire Pledge

You might call the Weekend Millionaire Pledge the last resort. If everything else has failed, we want you to take the Weekend Millionaire Pledge. Note the time on your watch, mentally raise your left hand, put your right hand over your heart, and say to yourself, "I hereby pledge that I will not leave these sellers for at least one more hour." Do whatever it takes, and even if you never mention your offer again, try to stay with them for one more hour.

You might ask for another cup of coffee—that'll take five minutes. Pretend it's too hot to drink and you can get ten minutes out of that. Maybe the pot is empty. That's good. Ask them if they will brew another one. Now you're talking half an hour. Whatever it takes, don't leave for one more hour.

This may sound strange, but we have learned that the longer you can keep the sellers engaged, the more flexible they become. Just because they're telling you no now doesn't mean that in 30 minutes they won't be saying maybe, and even yes in another 30 minutes.

When all else fails, take the Weekend Millionaire Pledge. Use a winning smile and a calm demeanor to draw the sellers closer. The more they come to like you, the better they will feel about doing business with you.

Key Points to Remember from This Chapter

- Closing tactics are techniques that salespeople use to get a buyer to make a decision faster than he or she otherwise would.
- A closing tactics does not cause sellers to accept an offer that they otherwise wouldn't. It just gets them to decide faster.
- The faster you can get the seller to decide, the better the chance you have of getting what you want.

Index

A

Acceptance of offer, 31–32,
    147–150
Address, locating property owners,
    58–61
Admit you don't know, 12–14, 157
All cash offer generation, 182–183
Alternative Choice Close, 203–204
American culture, 5, 151–154
Amiable personality style:
    described, 164–165
    difficulties with, 166
    negotiations with, 169
Analytical personality style:
    described, 165
    difficulties with, 167
    negotiations with, 169–170
Appraisers, county, 60–61
Arbitrator for deadlocks, 122,
    128–130

Arguing, avoiding in negotiating,
    92–94
Art of the Deal, The (Trump), 151
Ask questions (*See* Questioning)
Assertiveness dimension, seller
    personality styles, 160–161
Assessors, 60–61
Attitudinal negotiation style, 37–38
Auction sales of bank-owned
    properties, 42–45

B

Bank-owned properties, 39–46
    auction sales, 42–45
    cash deal, 41–42
    Internet information, 39–40
    pricing, 43–45
    through real estate
        agents/brokers, 40, 44
    title, 42

Index

Beginning negotiations
    (*See* Initial negotiations)
Ben Franklin Close, 197–199
Bidding war, Higher Authority
    Gambit, 107
Bond, Alan, 95–96
Bracketing as initial negotiating
    gambit, 86–88
Buyer's agency, 68–69
Buyer's agent, 62–64, 68–69

C

Cash deal:
    all cash offer generation,
        182–183
    bank-owned properties, 41–42
Chart of seller personality
    styles, 161
Christopher, Warren, 8
Clarifying question, Return Serve
    Close, 203
Closed-end questions, 19
Closing techniques, 189–210
    Alternative Choice Close,
        203–204
    Ben Franklin Close, 197–199
    Contingency Close, 197
    Divide and Conquer Close,
        205–207
    Doorknob Close, 205
    Dumb Mistake Close, 199–200
    Final Objection Close, 200–202
    Leave 'Em Alone Close, 193
    Let 'Em Think Close, 207–208
    Minor Point Close, 202
    Paddock Close, 191–192
    Recall Close, 208–209
    Return Serve Close, 203
    Silent Close, 195–196
    Subject-To Close, 111, 196–197
    Take Control Close, 209
    "That Wouldn't Stop You" Close,
        192–193

Tugboat Close, 189–191
Vince Lombardi Close, 194
Weekend Millionaire Pledge, 210
Commissions, real estate
    agents/brokers, 68–70, 72–73
Commitment to recommendation,
    Higher Authority Gambit,
    109–111
Communication, in foreign
    culture, 155
Competitive negotiation style, 33–34
Computers, Offer Generator
    program, 181–185, 187
Concessions:
    avoiding big final, 144–145
    bracketing, 87
    declining value of service,
        120–122
    tapering in concluding
        negotiations, 144–147
    as test, avoiding, 146
    time pressure, 25, 27–29
    Tugboat Close, 189–191
Concluding negotiations, 135–150
    concession tapering, 144–147
    Nibbling Gambit, 80–81, 135–141
    Positioning for Easy Acceptance
        Gambit, 147–150
    Withdrawing the Offer Gambit,
        141–144
Confrontational negotiation,
    avoiding, 92–94
Contingency Close, 197
Contracts:
    meaning of, foreign culture,
        152–153
    for purchase, 67–68
Counter Gambit:
    Higher Authority Gambit,
        108–112
    initial negotiating gambits, 99
    never say "yes" to first, 76–80
    Nibbling Gambit, 80–81, 135–141
County recorders, 60–61

Index

D

Deadlocks, 122, 128–130
Decision-making:
  Alternative Choice Close,
    203–204
  Contingency Close, 197
  Let 'Em Think Close, 207–208
  Minor Point Close, 202
  Take Control Close, 209
  Vince Lombardi Close, 194
  (*See also* Personality style of
    seller)
Declining value of service, 120–122
Development of personality
  styles, 159
Direct communication, in foreign
  culture negotiations, 155
Distractions, Paddock Close,
  191–192
Divide and Conquer Close, 205–207
Doing more than promised, win-win
  negotiating, 176–178
Doorknob Close, 205
Due diligence, real estate
  agents/brokers, 67
Dumb Mistake Close, 199–200

E

Easements, preliminary title
  report, 79
Ego, Higher Authority Gambit,
  109, 111
80/20 rule (Pareto principle), 24–25
Emerson, Ralph Waldo, xiii
Emotional considerations:
  foreign culture negotiations,
    156–157
  "house" vs. "home," 112–113
  seller personality styles, 160–161
Encumbrances, preliminary title
  report, 79
Ending negotiations (*See*
  Concluding negotiations)

Equal-sized concessions, avoiding,
  144
Extroverted personality style:
  described, 163–164
  difficulties with, 166–167
  negotiations with, 168–169

F

FAQs, Weekend Millionaire, xvi, 181
Federal Housing Administration
  (FHA), 47, 50–52
Feel, Felt, Found formula, 92–94
Feelings, asking for, 19–20
FHA (Federal Housing
  Administration), 47, 50–52
Fiduciary responsibility, real estate
  agents/brokers, 62, 67–68
Final Objective Close, 200–202
Financing:
  alternatives to conventional, xvii
  financed offer generation,
    Weekend Millionaire, 183–184
  win-win negotiating, 175
First offer, never say "yes" to,
  76–80
Flexibility, time pressure, 28–31
Flinch Gambit, 3–4
Flinch reaction, 88–91
For Sale By Owner (FSBO), 72, 96
Foreclosed properties:
  bank-owned, 39–46
  government-owned, 47–56
Foreign culture negotiations,
  151–158
  admit that you don't know, 157
  American focus on the deal,
    151–154
  American legal actions, 153–154
  contracts, 152–153
  direct communication, 155
  emotional displays, 156–157
  number of negotiators, 156
  outrageous initial demands, 155
  silence, 157

Index

Foreign culture negotiations (*Cont.*)
  stereotyping, 157–158
  talking business too quickly,
    154–155
Fortune, 11
Francis Xavier, St., 159
Franklin, Ben, 197–198
FSBO (For Sale By Owner), 72, 96

G

Gambits (*See* Negotiating gambits)
General Services Administration
  (GSA), 54
General Warranty Deed, 79
Giving you their problems, 115–120
Goals, win-win negotiating,
  174–176
Good Guy/Bad Guy, Higher
  Authority Gambit, 108
Good Neighbor Next Door Sales
  Programs, 52
Google, 59, 61
Government-owned properties,
  47–56
  FHA, 47, 50–52
  General Services Administration
    (GSA) sales, 54
  Internet information, 52–54
  seminar warning, 48–50
  sheriff's sales, 48, 53–54
  tax deed sales, 55
  tax lien sales, 54–55
  VA, 47–48, 51–53
Greed, avoiding, win-win
  negotiating, 176
GSA (General Services
  Administration), 54

H

Help me learn a lesson, Doorknob
  Close, 205
Hidden agenda, finding, 1–3, 12–22

Higher Authority Gambit, 103–112
Hippocrates, 160
Hot Potato, middle negotiating
  gambits, 115–120
"House" vs. "home," 112–113
HUD (U.S. Department of Housing
  and Urban Development), 47,
  50–51
Hussein, Saddam, 11–12

I

IFB (invitation for bid), 54
Impasse, middle negotiating
  gambits, 122–125
Information:
  admit you don't know, 12–14,
    157
  closed-end questions, 19
  hidden agenda, 1–3, 12–22
  initial position knowledge, 81
  listening skills, 11–12
  location for eliciting, 21–22
  open-ended questions, 18–20
  as power, 11–22
  pressures on other side, 1–3
Initial negotiations, 75–102
  ask for more that you expect to
    get, 80–86
  avoiding confrontational
    negotiation, 92–94
  bracketing, 86–88
  Counter Gambit, 99
  flinch reaction, to proposal,
    88–91
  never say "yes" to first
    offer/counteroffer, 76–80
  Reluctant Buyer Gambit,
    97–98
  Reluctant Seller Gambit, 94–97
  time, value of, 101–102
  Vise technique, 4, 98–102, 107
Inspection as negotiating tool,
  186–187

Index

Internet:
  bank-owned properties, 39–40
  FAQs, xvi, 181
  government-owned properties,
      52–54
  locating property owners, 59–60
  maps, 59
  online chats, 180–181
  Weekend Millionaire, xv,
      180–181
  Web site, xv
Investors:
  long-term investing tools,
      181–186
  as real estate agents/brokers,
      72–73
  working with real estate
      agents/brokers, 70–71
  (See also specific techniques)
Invitation for bid (IFB), 54
Issues vs. personalities,
      characteristics of power
      negotiator, 5–8

K

Kipling, Rudyard, 18–19
Knowledge (See Information)

L

Land, as investment, 77
Leases and rentals, 25–27, 77
  (See also specific topics)
Leave door open, 10
Leave 'Em Alone Close, 193
Left-brain thinking, 125612
Let 'Em Think Close, 207–208
Letters of intent, 184–186
Lis Pendens, preliminary title
      report, 79
Listening skills, 11–12
Listing pros and cons, Ben Franklin
      Close, 197–199

Locating property owner (See
      Property owners, locating)
Location for asking questions,
      21–22
Long-term investing tools, for
      offers, 181–186

M

Maps, Internet, 59
Mathematics of investment, xvi
Maximum plausible position (MPP),
      81–82
Mediator, deadlocks, 122, 128–130
Middle negotiations, 103–133
  Counter Gambit, 108–112
  deadlocks, 122, 128–130
  declining value of service,
      120–122
  gives you their problems, 115–120
  Higher Authority Gambit,
      103–112
  Hot Potato, 115–120
  impasse, 122–125
  Set-Aside Gambit, 123–124
  Split the Difference, 112–115
  stalemates, 122, 125–128
  Trade-Off Gambit, 131–133
Minor Point Close, 202
MPP (maximum plausible position),
      81–82
Multiple issues, in win-win
      negotiating, 173–174

N

Napoleon Bonaparte, 77
Negotiating:
  beginning, 75–102
  ending, 135–150
  foreign cultures, 151–158
  middle (See Middle negotiations)
  offers, and investing tools,
      181–186

Index

Negotiating (*Cont.*)
"power negotiator," 1–10
practice, 3–5
range of, 89–90
seller personality styles,
167–170
strategy with real estate
agents/brokers, 73–74
style of, 33–38
win-win, 171–178
Negotiating gambits:
concluding, 135–150
defined, 75
initial, 75–102
middle, 103–133
(*See also specific gambits*)
Negotiators, number of, foreign
culture, 156
Neighbors, 58
Net operating income (NOI), 182
Net realizable value (NRV), 44–45
Nibble Gambit, 80–81, 135–141
"No" as opening position,
characteristics of power
negotiator, 8–10
NOI (net operating income), 182
NRV (net realizable value), 44–45

O

Objections:
Final Objective Close, 200–202
Higher Authority Gambit,
110–111
"That Wouldn't Stop You" Close,
192–193
Ocwen Loan Servicing LLC, 52–53
Offer(s):
acceptance, 31–32, 147–150
FAQs, 181
inspection as tool, 186–187
meet seller's needs, 179–188
online chats, 180–181
wholesale, 71

Offer Generator program, 181–185,
187
Online chats, 180–181
Open-ended questions, 18–20
Organizational negotiation style,
36–37
Outrageous initial demands, foreign
culture, 155
Owner-occupation, FHA, 50
Owners of property (*See* Property
owners, locating)

P

Paddock Close, 191–192
Pareto, Vilfredo, 24
Pareto principle (80/20 rule),
24–25
Partners or spouses
Divide and Conquer Close,
205–207
Higher Authority Gambit,
106–108
Leave 'Em Alone Close, 193
PBS (Public Building Service), 54
Perception of winning, win-win
negotiating, 173
Performance, win-win negotiating,
175
Personality style of seller:
Amiable, 164–166, 169
Analytical, 165–167,
169–170
assertiveness dimension,
160–161
development, 159
difficulties presented by,
166–167
emotional dimension, 160–161
Extroverted, 163–164,
166–169
negotiations, 167–170
vs. power negotiator, 5–8
Pragmatic, 162–163, 166–168

Index

Positioning for Easy Acceptance
Gambit, 147–150
"Power negotiator" characteristics
American cultural reluctance to
negotiate, 5
finding seller's hidden agenda,
1–3, 12–22
issues vs. personalities, 5–8
leave the door open, 10
"no" as opening position, 8–10
practice skills in inconsequential
situations, 3–5
Practice negotiation, 3–5
Pragmatic personality style
described, 162–163
difficulties with, 166
negotiations with, 167–168
Preliminary title report, 78–79
Pressure, finding seller's hidden
agenda, 1–3, 12–22
Price:
bank-owned properties, 43–45
negotiating range, 89
for offers, 181–186
time pressure, 24, 29–31
(*See also specific topics*)
Priestly, Joseph, 197–198
Problem resolution, time pressure,
24–25, 31
Property managers, Higher
Authority Gambit, 106
Property owners, locating, 57–65
address of property owners,
58–61
conforming area, 58
Internet information, 59–60
local information sites, 61
neighbors, 58
nonconforming area, 58
owner name unknown, 60–61
preliminary title report, 78–79
public records, 61
real estate agents, 62–64
title companies, 61–62

Pros and cons, Ben Franklin Close,
197–199
Public Building Service (PBS), 54
Public records, 61
Purchase contracts, 67–68

Q

Questioning:
clarifying, Return Serve Close,
203
finding seller's hidden agenda,
14–22
information as power, 19
initial negotiating gambits,
80–86
open-ended questions, 18–20

R

Reactions, asking for, 20
Real estate agents/brokers, 67–74
bank-owned properties, 40, 44
buyer's agent, 68–69
as buyers agents, 62–64
commissions, 68–70, 72–73
due diligence, 67
fiduciary responsibility, 62,
67–68
finding a great one, 70–71
and FSBOs, 72
investors as, 72–73
locating property owners, 62–64
negotiating offer, 96
negotiating strategy with, 73–74
promissory notes in lieu of
commission, 73
and purchase contracts, 67–68
selling agent, 68, 73
subagency, 68–69
wholesale offers, 71
working with investors, 70–71
as working for themselves, 70
Recall Close, 208–209

Index

Recommendation, Higher Authority Gambit, 109–111
Reluctant Buyer Gambit, 97–98
Reluctant Seller Gambit, 94–97
Rentals and leases, 25–27, 77
  (*See also specific topics*)
REO (real estate owned) properties
  (*See* Bank-owned properties)
Repeat the comment as question, 19–20
Resistance, Vince Lombardi Close, 194
Restatement, asking for, 20
Return Serve Close, 203
Richardson, Bill, 11, 83
Right-brain thinking, 161

S

St. Francis Xavier, 159
"Secrets of Power Negotiating" seminar, 89–90
Sellers (*See* Personality style of seller; *specific topics*)
Selling agent, real estate agents/brokers, 68, 73
Seminars, xii, xv, 2, 48–50
  (*See also* Weekend Millionaire)
Service, declining value of, 120–122
Set-Aside Gambit, 123–124
Sheriff's sales, government-owned properties, 48, 53–54
Side with most options, time pressure, 25–26
Silence:
  foreign culture negotiations, 157
  negotiations, 100–101
  Silent Close, 195–196
Solutional negotiation style, 34–36
Split the Difference Gambit, 112–115
Spouses (*See* Partners or spouses)
Stalemates, 122, 125–128
Stereotyping, foreign cultures, 157–158

Style of negotiation, 33–38
  attitudinal, 37–38
  competitive, 33–34
  organizational, 36–37
  personal, 36
  solutional, 34–36
Subagency, 68–69
Subject-To Close, 111, 196–197

T

Take Control Close, 209
Talking business too quickly, American culture, 154–155
Tax assessors, 60–61
Tax deed sales, 55
Tax lien sales, 54–55
Tennis game analogy, 6
Terms (*See specific topics*)
Test for validity, Hot Potato, 116–120
"That Wouldn't Stop You" Close, 192–193
Third party, deadlocks, 122, 128–130
Time:
  acceptance time, 31–32
  both sides have same deadline, 25–27
  concessions, 25, 27–29
  examples of, 24
  flexibility, 28–31
  Pareto principle (80/20 rule), 24–25
  pressure of, 23–32
  problem resolution, 24–25, 31
  property price variation, 24, 29–31
  side with most options, 25–26
  value of, initial negotiating gambits, 101–102
Title, bank-owned properties, 42
Title companies, 61–62
Title insurance, 78–79

Title report, preliminary, 78–79
Trade-Off Gambit, 131–133
Trump, Donald, 29, 95, 151
Tugboat Close, 189–191

U

Unilateral Disarmament, 145–146
U.S. Department of Agriculture
   (USDA), 53
U.S. Department of Housing and
   Urban Development (HUD),
   47, 50–51
U.S. Department of Veteran Affairs
   (VA), 47–48, 51–53
Upset bids, 45
USDA (U.S. Department of
   Agriculture), 53

V

VA (U.S. Department of Veteran
   Affairs), 47–48, 51–53
Value:
   defined, 23
   of service, declining, 120–122
Vince Lombardi Close, 194
Vise Gambit, 4, 98–102, 107
Vulnerability, Nibbling Gambit,
   138–139

W

Weekend Millionaire, 180–187
   all cash offer generation,
      182–183
   described, xiv, xv-xvi
   FAQs, xvi, 181
   financed offer generation,
      183–184

inspection form, 186–187
investment philosophy, xvi-xvii
letters of intent, 184–186
long-term investing tools,
   181–186
net operating income (NOI), 182
Offer Generator program,
   181–185, 187
online chats, 180–181
Pledge, 210
Weekend Millionaire Mindset, The
   (Summey and Dawson), xiii-xv
*Weekend Millionaire Offer
   Generator,* 43
*Weekend Millionaire's Secrets to
   Investing in Real Estate, The*
   (Summey and Dawson), xi-xii,
   xv, 18, 36, 43–44, 62, 94,
   179–180
Wholesale offers, 71
Williams & Williams Marketing
   Services, Inc., 42
Win-win negotiating, 171–178
   avoid greed, 176
   different goals, 174–176
   doing more than promised,
      176–178
   keep multiple issues, 173–174
   perception of winning to other
      side, 173
Winning, perception of, to other
   side, 173
Withdrawing the Offer Gambit,
   141–144
Women, as negotiators, 2

Z

Zillow Website, 59

About the Authors

Mike Summey (Asheville, NC) is a multimillionaire real estate investor with over 34 years of experience in buying income producing properties. He writes a weekly newspaper column titled "Weekend Millionaire Tips for Financial Success," is a frequent guest on numerous radio shows, and conducts live seminars around the country.

Roger Dawson (LaHabra Heights, CA) is one of the country's top experts in the art of negotiating. *Success* magazine calls him "America's premier business negotiator." As a full-time speaker since 1982, he has trained managers and salespeople at the top companies and business associations throughout the United States, Canada, Europe, and Australia. He was inducted into the Speaker Hall of Fame in 1991.

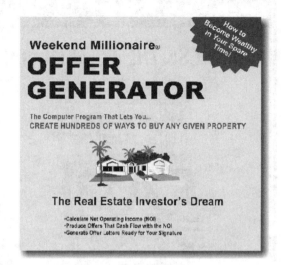

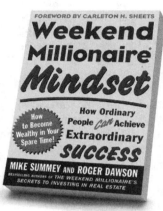